CRY OF THE OPPRESSED

BY ROBERT F. DRINAN, S.J.

God and Caesar on the Potomac: A Pilgrimage of Conscience (*1985*)

Beyond the Nuclear Freeze (*1983*)

Honor the Promise: America's Commitment to Israel (*1977*)

Vietnam and Armageddon (*1970*)

Democracy, Dissent, and Disorder (*1969*)

Religion, the Courts, and Public Policy (*1963*)

CRY
OF THE
OPPRESSED

The History and Hope
of the Human Rights Revolution

ROBERT F. DRINAN, S.J.

1817

Harper & Row, Publishers, San Francisco

Cambridge, Hagerstown, New York, Philadelphia, Washington
London, Mexico City, São Paulo, Singapore, Sydney

CRY OF THE OPPRESSED: *The History and Hope of the Human Rights Revolution*. Copyright © 1987 by the Society of Jesus of New England. All rights reserved. Printed in the United States of America. No part of this book may be used or reproduced in any manner whatsoever without written permission except in the case of brief quotations embodied in critical articles and reviews. For information address Harper & Row, Publishers, Inc., 10 East 53rd Street, New York, NY 10022. Published simultaneously in Canada by Fitzhenry & Whiteside, Limited, Toronto.

FIRST EDITION

Library of Congress Cataloging-in-Publication Data

Drinan, Robert F.
  Cry of the oppressed.

  Bibliography: p.
  Includes index.
  1. Human rights—History. I. Title.
K3240.4.D74   1987   342'.085   87-45173
ISBN 0-06-250261-1   342.285

87 88 89 90 91 RRD 10 9 8 7 6 5 4 3 2 1

Contents

Preface

The defense of internationally recognized human rights has become the most universally accepted moral standard in the world today. Across the ideological spectrum, from the far left to the far right, there is agreement that the one unifying spiritual ideal in modern society is the enhancement and enforcement of human rights.

The centrality of human rights is so pervasive an idea in contemporary society that few are aware how recently this moral framework became a part of the world of the late twentieth century. Actually it is a recent revolution, dating only from the formation of the United Nations and the promulgation by that body of some two dozen covenants, or treaties, on human rights. The very idea that international law would give protection to *individual* human rights is so new it is startling. International law has always been quite literally a body of law regarding the relations of nations to each other. The rights of individuals have never been a part of the law of nations. But World War II changed all of that. The slaughter of thirty-five million people and the genocidal death in the Holocaust of six million Jews forced the Allied powers and the rest of humanity to internationalize the emerging law that makes human rights sacred and inviolable.

The human rights law that has flowered over the last forty years operates at the official level and, sometimes more importantly, at the level of the ever more numerous nongovernmental organizations devoted to human rights. This volume tries to tell the story of how the double revolution of official and unofficial action on behalf of human rights is arousing and changing the world. This is a book filled with law, experiences, and hope. It is not overly optimistic, since law is a frail instrument against institutionalized avarice and organized self-interest. But it is nonetheless a book filled with hope, since both human rights bureaucrats and human rights nongovernmental activists are combining their efforts to make freedom and equality a reality for millions.

As a professor at Georgetown University Law Center since 1981, each year I have taught a class of 130 students in international human rights. The development of the law in that area is almost amazing. And the number of lawyers and activists engaged in the promotion of human rights is constantly increasing. Consequently by the year 2000 the ways in which human rights are respected and enforced across the world may be dramatically strengthened. In order to attain that hoped-for objective at least a small army of well-informed persons must work to define, enhance, and protect the rights of all human beings. This book is written to help to produce that small army. It seeks to describe and defend the legal, moral, spiritual, and religious roots of the human rights revolution. I hope it will inform and inspire many people to recognize that countless men, women, and even children around the world are oppressed and crushed by dictatorships of the right and of the left. To those victims of authoritarian and totalitarian injustice this book is dedicated.

INTRODUCTION: THE UNIVERSAL CRY FOR HUMAN RIGHTS

Across the world a new gospel is echoing in the hearts of men and women—the good news that their human rights are recognized and somehow guaranteed by the law of nations. It is a rather recent realization among the oppressed of the world. But since this novel idea was first promoted in the Charter of the United Nations (1945), it has entered the consciousness of humankind and has become one of the great driving forces of the modern world.

The concept that the protection of the fundamental human rights of every person transcends local and national law is an earth-shaking idea like the abolition of slavery, the phasing out of colonialism, and the abolition of apartheid. While the enforceability of human rights around the world is more than a dream but less than a reality, it is everywhere the principal aspiration of dissidents and insurgents. It is also the central concern of jurists and activists who yearn to bring liberation and dignity to those nations where freedom, democracy, and human rights are not protected.

The deep anxiety for the guarantees of human rights takes form in a wide variety of ways. It can be seen in Chile, where every year on September 11 thousands of people crowd the plazas and the parks of Santiago to protest the theft of their liberties on September 11, 1973, when General Augusto Pinochet seized power and President Salvador Allende was killed. The crowds in Chile know they will face tear gas and water cannons, but they simply have to express their pain that their nation, with a long and venerable adherence to democracy, is now dominated by one of the world's cruelest dictators.

The same determination can be seen in the demands of El Salvadoran peasants for land reform. I recall concelebrating a late evening mass outside of San Salvador for a group of farm workers who expressed in their offertory petitions the pain and humiliation that they daily experienced. One middle-aged man articulated his anger at the fact that the government of El Salvador—made up of the fourteen families that have controlled that country for many decades—appropriated the land of his great-grandfather. He affirmed that he would not rest until he had recaptured that land for his children and his grandchildren. I remember on another occasion the spontaneous applause when I spoke the words *derechos humanos* in a sermon in the cathedral in San Salvador. On still another occasion in Guatemala the local bishop thanked me for preaching about human rights, explaining that if he himself addressed such a topic, the government might well deport twelve of his priests who were not citizens of Guatemala.

I recall the anguish for human rights that I experienced during the hearings in which I participated as a member of a team visiting Argentina in November 1976 on behalf of Amnesty International. That country had been traumatized by a military takeover on March 24, 1976. Thousands of people died or disappeared in the "dirty war" waged by the military government against the Monteneros and other alleged subversives. One of the first persons I met in Argentina was Dr. Emilio Mignone, a former university president and ambassador. His daughter Monica was taken from her home early in the morning by four plainclothesmen who claimed to be law enforcement officers. She never returned. Monica's case and those of 8,960 other individuals were written up in the annals of the seven-year war in *Nunca Mas (Never Again)*. This volume, a bestseller in Argentina now translated into English, is another dramatic indication of the depth of feeling for human rights in Argentina and around the world. The publicly appointed commission that produced this study wanted to document what the top officials of Argentina did during its dark night. One of the effects of the study was the conviction and imprisonment of some of Argentina's highest military officials.

The same aspiration for liberation sparked the Helsinki groups, that sprang up all over Eastern Europe after thirty-five nations, including the USSR and the United States, signed the Helsinki accords on August 1, 1975. Despite discouragement and even severe penalties imposed on them by the Kremlin, the Helsinki dissenters continued their activities. The very idea of human rights has energized and electrified them.

Many moral themes underline the ever-deepening consensus that fundamental human rights should and can be observed. One of these themes is the presence in the constitutions and basic laws of some one hundred new nations of the ideas, indeed the very language, of the United Nations charter and the political and economic rights that this world organization has promulgated and popularized.

The lasting power of a moral idea should never be underestimated. It took generations, even centuries, for the ideals of the Magna Carta adopted at Runnymede in the year 1215 to be accepted in England and in the scores of nations to which English law was extended. So too the moral ideas inherent in the nineteen major covenants, or treaties, that have emerged from the United Nations will require some time to be accepted. But the instantaneous communication of ideas and news around the world has made it possible, perhaps even inevitable, that the exultation of human rights, which is at the core of everything the United Nations stands for, will continue to command the attention of the world's five billion inhabitants. It is an idea whose time has come.

Another compelling theme in the contemporary surge of interest in human rights is the hope that guaranteeing human rights will reduce or even eliminate racism. The colonial powers—England, France, Spain, Portugal, Holland, and others—built their empires in Africa and Asia on the assertion of the superiority of the white race. Many of the black, brown, and yellow people of the world accepted that classification until, after decades, they realized that they had been victimized and exploited, a realization that led to the revolutions that caused the collapse of colonialism after World War II. But even more important to the increasing concern for human rights was the anger and indignation of nonwhite peoples everywhere; that anger led to the authorship of the seminal United Nations covenants exalting human rights. These documents helped to produce or to finalize the revolt of the nations of Africa and Asia.

The only one of the fifty-one nations of Africa that has not yet decolonized is South Africa and it is to that segregated nation that

Africa and the whole world have devoted their energy. Apartheid has been condemnd by the United Nations Security Council, the General Assembly, the International Court of Justice (the World Court) at The Hague, and every political and private human rights agency in the world. The institution of apartheid unites every aspirant for human rights around the world. The global condemnation of Pretoria in 1987 reflected the culmination of all the frustrations of the postcolonial nations that for decades were humiliated by the racism invented and institutionalized by the European powers. The drumbeat against South Africa will not cease because the fact that twenty-six million blacks are segregated and deprived of their citizenship only because they are black is intolerable to all who affirm human rights.

The International Convention on the Elimination of All Forms of Racial Discrimination (1969) has been ratified by 129 nations—more nations than have ratified any other UN treaty. Its language is strong. It equates racism with "hatred." It represents the outcry of millions of people whose ancestors were kept in subjugation by the colonial conquerors. This document by its very existence—aside from its enforcement—sums up most of what the Third World is trying to tell the developed nations and the rest of humanity.

OBSTACLES TO HUMAN RIGHTS GUARANTEES

But our contemporary enthusiasm for human rights should not blind us to the enormous obstacles that still stand in the way of protecting these rights. The most Solomon-like judge is not likely to resolve right away the Israeli-Arab confrontations. Human rights are not a panacea that can dissolve the decades-long differences between peoples. Political adversaries have to accept the status of litigants before law can settle their differences. In addition, they must agree to accept the result of litigation even if they lose.

Nevertheless, establishing that certain truths or norms of an international character are binding on individual states is in itself a great leap forward. Even if such norms do not now seem to be universally acceptable or enforceable, their mere existence teaches that the rule of law is attainable. By establishing universal and globally accepted criteria for human rights seeks to break down or transcend the barriers that have kept nations and peoples apart. While we can exult that jurists and diplomats have conceived a formula for world peace, we must also admit that people in particular nations, conditioned by centuries of provincialism and group prejudice, are not necessarily prepared as yet to have their prepossessions set aside by an international tribunal. Powerful cultural differences have not been amendable to those legal processes utilized for disputes between parties with common cultural backgrounds.

Without question, however, the elevation of human rights to the international level is one of the most dramatic events in the entire history of jurisprudence. It will have consequences and implications that even the most sanguine observer of human rights cannot now foresee. The growth of international law with respect to human rights can be compared with the evolution of federal law with respect to state law in the United States. The framers of the federal Constitution specifically ruled that matters related to immigration, copyright, patents, and bankruptcy would be exclusively governed by federal law. The commerce clause in the Constitution, which authorizes Congress to regulate commerce between the states, has allowed Congress the broadest possible mandate to regulate those rights deemed to be rights for all citizens of the United States. Thus federal protection of certain rights overrides state laws.

The same process has been in effect since the signing of the United Nations charter. All of the UN human rights covenants have extended international protection to certain rights so fundamental they deserve recognition by world law, not just by individual nations. The concept is bold, daring, almost utopian. It was the product of emotional outrage at the devastation wrought by World War II. But this concept also resulted from decades of development of international law that urged the recognition that human rights are too precious to be at the mercy of authoritarian or totalitarian despots.

Those skeptical of the force of law may quite properly object that it is naive and unrealistic to think that world law can help the Moslems in Mindanao, the survivors of the atrocities at My Lai, or political prisoners in remote sections of China. But such skepticism fails to recognize that for the first time in the history of the human race 160 nations have agreed that international law, binding on all nations, guarantees individuals the right of recourse if their countries violate specific fundamental rights. Even if the details about the enforceability of this new and amazing right of recourse are not yet settled, the recognition of rights that eventually will be juridically enforceable has incalculable consequences.

Laws and courts have a way of eventually making possible the enforcement of rights. Sir Hersch Lauterpacht, the great international legal scholar, wrote in an era before the acceptance of the idea that human rights should be protected by world law. Nonetheless, he asserted that the moral rights of today are very often the legal rights of tomorrow.

But, it can be argued, the protection of the rights guaranteed by the UN charter and the treaties that derive from it are not really earth-shattering since they are only political rights and not economic rights, which millions of sick and chronically malnourished people are denied. The figures on the deprivation of economic rights are staggering, indeed sickening. Some eight hundred million persons—one-sixth of humanity—are regularly underfed. Up to forty thousand children die each day of preventable causes. The predicted world population in the year 2000 is 6.2 billion. Unfortunately it cannot be stated that the 1.2 billion who will be added to the population of the Earth during the 1990s will be better off than the disadvantaged today. This enormous tragedy is deepened by the irony that the resources of the world, if properly allocated, could furnish adequate food, medicine, and clothing for all of humanity.

Why not concentrate on the important rights, the rights to food, to shelter, and to economic security? The socialist nations proposed precisely that when the United Nations was working on the development of the covenants to spell out the commitments made in the UN charter. But the capitalist nations resisted. The result was the separation of political from economic rights and the writing of two separate covenants. Both covenants have, by reason of a sufficient number of ratifications, now entered into international law. But the emphasis on political rights by the developed nations and the exaltation of economic rights by the Soviet bloc and the Third World have undoubtedly weakened the implementation of both sets of rights. As a result the nations of the North—capitalist countries—appear to the South—the undeveloped nations—to be concentrating excessively on political rights, such as the right not to be detained by the government without being charged with a crime, but neglecting economic rights, such as the right to have an income adequate for one's family.

No major nation or international agency has suggested that the United Nations or its affiliated human rights organizations give up the emphasis on political rights in order to stress economic rights. But what the Third World perceives to be the insincerity or hypocrisy of the rich nations clearly diminishes the desire of the underdeveloped nations to emphasize and enforce political rights when their economic rights are so neglected. This situation has been aggravated by the enormous debts to the First World accumulated by the Third World over the past fifteen years. The leaders of the developing nations would much prefer to have some relief from their burdensome debts than to hear more lectures about their countries' shortcomings concerning the full attainment of political rights.

This embarrassing posture of the rich nations is acutely so in the case of the United States, which, unlike all other major nations, has not ratified either the political or economic covenants promulgated by the United Nations. Consequently the slow progress made in developing human rights guarantees worldwide must be attributed in part—perhaps in large part—to the United States, which, though it was the principal leader in developing the United Nations, can be seen as having abandoned its role of leadership soon after the United Nations was formed in 1945 and the UN Universal Declaration of Human Rights was agreed to unanimously on December 10, 1948.

Although jurists and human rights activists can rejoice about the golden age for human rights that the world has seen for four decades, they have to admit that the hungry in Brazil, the refugees in Africa, and the street beggars in Calcutta cannot be expected to believe that a great revolution has occurred. These unfortunate individuals have a right to think that world law has passed them by.

It is interesting to speculate what might have happened if the rich and the poor nations, both tormented and victimized by the East-West rivalry in the United Nations, had managed to keep the political and economic rights in one document that now would be binding in international law for the entire world. Both the political and economic covenants are a part of world law, but the United Nations Commission on Human Rights and regional tribunals on human rights have given almost their total attention to the enforcement of political rights.

The rich nations, in other words, have to some extent distorted the purpose and unity of the United Nations charter by insisting on separating political from economic rights. By so doing, the nations of the First World have appeared to be imposing on the Third World those political rights that are taken for granted in developed nations. But in the process they have neglected the fulfillment of economic rights that are so desperately desired in the world of poorer nations and destitute people.

The same division in the family of nations has occurred when the poor countries have pleaded at the United Nations, and in any other forum available to them, for a new international economic order. The United States and most capitalist nations have rejected this appeal or are at least perceived to have done so. In the early 1980s the rejection was accompanied by lectures about the value of free enterprise and the "magic of the marketplace."

But despite the tragic differences that exist in the thinking of the rich and the poor nations, no one can deny the monumental significance of the fact that international law flowered more in the past forty years than it did in the previous forty centuries. International law has stated that human rights are so precious and sacred that not even sovereign nations can crush them. If a nation does violate what the UN charter calls "human rights and fundamental freedoms," that nation can be judged to be in violation of international law. Even though the means for punishing such a violation have not yet been determined, humankind has attained a new level of sophistication by the solemn declaration that some rights are so undeniable and inviolable that their infringement demands atonement.

One of the more difficult problems inherent in international protection of an array of human rights now is the ultimate philosophical reason given for that protection. Those who believe that God has revealed himself to humankind would have preferred that the UN charter contain some acknowledgment of this faith or at least of the contribution and relevance of this faith to the growth of reverence for human rights. But the UN charter does not mention revealed religion or indeed any theistic commitment. It does not specify that nations are under God. It only states that nations are under the law. It does utilize several key concepts derived more from the Judeo-Christian tradition than from other religions, and the religious origins of these concepts—for example, the notion of fraternity endorsed by the UN charter—are clear and undeniable. But the UN charter assumes that the devotion to human rights that it stresses can be effective and enforceable from notions less than theistic although concededly more than pragmatic or utilitarian. To date there has been no rejection of the charter as a document based allegedly on secularism or humanism. But the charter does not coincide with the theistic underpinnings of the government of so many nations, especially in the Arab world. The UN charter assumes that there is enough conviction and consensus in the entire world about the value of human rights that all nations, whether their governments have a sacred or secular orientation, can adhere to the charter and carry out its mandates.

That assumption has not been openly challenged by any of the one hundred nations who did not participate in the founding of the United Nations because they were not then independent countries. The closest that such nations have come to a challenge to the entire UN structure is their charge that the developed nations that drafted the charter do not actually believe in its values, especially those that speak of the right to economic equality. But a strong case can be made that the UN charter and the legal institutions that have developed as its enforcement arm are compatible and indeed supportive of all the major moral beliefs and practices of the religions of the world. This is true especially with respect to human rights. In every moral and legal system certain values are considered absolute and cannot be subverted for any cause, however appealing. In any civilized nation these values will be generally safeguarded. By incorporation or reference the UN charter has embraced some of the best thought of Aristotle, St. Thomas

Aquinas, John Locke, and the framers of the United States Declaration of Independence. Can the philosophical premises of this long Western tradition embracing natural law and human rights support and develop a world law that will be acceptable to countries and continents with far different traditions? The complete answer is not as yet ascertainable. Because the UN charter evades certain difficult central questions, the decisions of the UN agencies created to carry out its mandates may not be universally accepted. But it can be persuasively argued that in the forty years since World War II the human rights approach so central to the United Nations has attained a remarkable level of acceptance and enforcement in a world torn asunder by East-West and North-South differences and disputes.

As the proponents of human rights treaties hope, there may be a moral consensus among nations to make the universal acceptance of the sanctity of human rights a permanent and irreversible part of the law of nations.

THE ROLE OF NONGOVERNMENTAL ORGANIZATIONS

The founders of the United Nations expected that it would be very difficult for nations to yield a part of their sovereignty in order to protect the human rights of individuals. Nations are as jealous of their sovereignty and their majesty as they were centuries ago when the nation-state first came into existence. When the United Nations formulated standards for the international protection of human rights, it knew that it was asking nations to make sacrifices they had never before been asked to make. Knowing how difficult this would be, the United nations expressly embraced the mission and work of the many nongovernmental organizations (NGOs). From its very beginning the United Nations endorsed NGOs and sought their close collaboration. When the UN charter was being formulated at San Francisco in 1945, there were forty-two nongovernmental organizations present. These organizations went there to strengthen the draft of the UN charter that had emerged from Dumbarton Oaks in 1944. They succeeded. The value of human rights is mentioned expressly in seven different places in the UN charter even though, amazingly, human rights were not mentioned in the documents related to the League of Nations. Nongovernmental organizations can take credit for the heavy accent on human rights in the UN charter.

Nongovernmental organizations are therefore almost an inherent or organic complement to the United Nations. The number of these organizations has increased very significantly since 1945. Today, following the lead of Amnesty International, which was founded in London in 1961, dozens of NGOs are devoted to human rights. The growth and dynamism of these groups is an inherent and important part of the amazing story of how the sanctity and inviolability of all human rights became a part of international law. The NGOs are concerned wherever complaints are made about tyranny or torture. NGOs are depositories of information, communicators of bad news, and bearers of hope for those who are oppressed. NGOs have been called private attorneys general. They investigate and indict tyrants in public opinion. They are an essential component of that moral revolution in favor of human rights that has exploded across the world in the years after World War II.

The prominence of NGOs would not have been possible if international law had not changed so that the violation of the human rights of the most obscure person in the most forgotten country is a violation of world law. The mission of the NGOs is predicated on the existence of international recognition of human rights. When dreadful abuses occurred in the years before the United Nations came into being, individuals and public interest groups undoubtedly protested. But their protest was based on a humanitarian or idealistic basis; they had no international law to which why could appeal. This is now entirely changed. Those who report and rebuke the violations of human rights can appeal to the highest levels of power because they are complaining about a violation of world law.

NGOs such as Amnesty International, the International Commission of Jurists, and the Lawyers Committee for Human Rights often seek to dramatize the cases they adopt. Amnesty International, with its five hundred thousand members in every country of the world, "adopts" political prisoners and besieges the governments that detain them to release these people. It appeals to world opinion on the assumption that the abuse that has occurred violates world law.

The NGOs are the new abolitionists. Around the year 1800 individuals and groups, largely church related, began the long process of convincing the American people that they could not in conscience live in a nation that retained slavery as an institution. The founders of the abolitionist movement probably never dreamed that their crusade would take sixty-five years to accomplish. When the British empire abolished slavery throughout the Commonwealth in 1883, the abolitionists hoped that the United States Congress would soon follow. When four million slaves of African origin were finally emancipated, a nation and a world praised and practically canonized those who had sacrificed so much over such a long period of time to rid America of a curse.

The NGOs of today are imitating the practices and the persistence of the abolitionists. But human rights activists today have an enormous advantage not available to the abolitionists—the denial of those rights recognized in the documents of the United Nations is already a violation of world law. NGOs in today's world therefore are not seeking to create a law as the abolitionists were but are seeking to enforce a law already binding on every sovereign nation.

Private human rights groups such as Americas Watch, Freedom House, and the International League for Human Rights seek to call attention to the abuses they report by dramatizing the terrible personal tragedies involved. Deprivation of human rights in Chile, Zaire, Indonesia, and Sri Lanka violates a law binding on the United States and the entire world. To be silent or inactive about human rights abuses anywhere is therefore to involve us in misprision, the crime of not reporting crimes, or, even worse, to make us accomplices in the theft of a person's most precious possessions, his or her human rights.

An American citizen would find it hard to discover an excuse for not doing what can be done to prevent the carrying out of arson or rape. An American or any person of any nation could easily discover moral values that impel him or her to report crime or anticipate crime. Now that the world has in effect criminalized the denial by any state of internationally recognized human rights, no citizen of the world can justify unconcern or silence about crimes figuratively being committed in our presence.

The NGOs recognize all of this and are organized to carry out the New World responsibilities of every member of the human race. The moral and spiritual forces that created the NGOs are the same forces that brought the United Nations and the agencies associated with it into existence. The international machinery established by the United Nations would not have come into existence without the private human rights organizations around the world. Nor can that machinery be expected to develop or even, perhaps, to survive without the active and durable collaboration of persons and groups who feel hurt when any other human being is hurt.

Caring about the violations of human rights has of course been for centuries one of those lovely human characteristics that give rise to the hope that the morality of humankind is not declining but might be improving. Solon, the ancient Athenian jurist, said it well when he declared that justice will not come until those who are not hurt feel just as indignant as those who are hurt.

Caring for others on an international scale was not totally unknown before World War II. One of the first recorded instances in which one nation used persuasion and sanctions to protect the human rights of others occurred in the year 480 B.C. Gelon, the prince of Syracuse, having defeated Carthage, made it a condition of peace that the Carthaginians abandon their time-honored custom of sacrificing their children to Saturn.

One might also say that Moses was the first human rights activist when he pleaded to Pharoah to let his people go. Because Egypt was plagued in countless ways, Pharoah finally yielded to the pleas of the Israelites. Today the plea of world law and the ever more numerous armies of those who seek to carry it out is an appeal to the law, binding on the whole world, that turns every act that denies a human right into a crime. This appeal is powerful and imperious.

I. THE HEART OF THE HUMAN RIGHTS REVOLUTION

1. The United Nations Emphasis on Human Rights

When the League of Nations was formed in 1919 it was almost unthinkable that an international organization could proclaim that the violation of the human rights of any one person or group could be made into a violation of international law. At the time only slavery and piracy were violations of international law, and the process by which these offenses were proscribed by international law took decades, even centuries. But the League of Nations, although it enunciated its concern for minorities and expressed interest in the welfare of people in colonized nations, took bold action on one matter directly related to human rights. It established the International Labor Organization (ILO), which was the first international governmental agency in the world created to define and vindicate human rights. In the decades of its existence the ILO has promulgated hundreds of standards to improve the conditions of working men and women around the world. Although it seeks voluntary rather than compelled compliance, it has had an extraordinary influence on the lives of millions. In 1969 the ILO received the Nobel Peace Price for its work on behalf of human rights.

THE UNITED NATIONS CHARTER

When work began on the organization of the United Nations during World War II there was at first no deep interest in highlighting the observance of human rights. The main thrust was, as the preamble of the charter notes, to save the world "from the scourge of war." But the document that was accepted at Dumbarton Oaks in 1944 was changed substantially at the San Francisco Conference. Peace and human rights groups born in the 1920s and 1930s were determined to strengthen the UN charter on the question of human rights. At San Francisco a group of forty-two nongovernmental agencies assumed almost a confrontational role with representatives of the United States State Department. These representatives, like their counterparts around the world, wanted to preserve the sovereignty of nations as they had known it throughout their careers. They were not about to concede that the violation of individual human rights within one nation could turn that nation into a violator of international law. But those advocating the protection of human rights as one of the top objectives of the United Nations prevailed. The idea of human rights is mentioned seven times in the UN charter. The second of the four clauses in the preamble of the charter is the reaffirmation of faith "in fundamental human rights, in the dignity and worth of the human person, in the equal rights of men and women and of nations large and small." The four purposes and top principles of the United Nations set forth in Article 1 of the charter include that of "promoting and encouraging respect for human rights and for fundamental freedoms for all without distinction as to race, sex, language, or religion."

Articles 55 and 56 make it clear, moreover, that all of the signatories of the UN charter "pledge themselves to take joint and separate action" to "promote . . . universal respect for, and observance of, human rights and fundamental freedoms for all without distinction as to race, sex, language or religion." Both this language and the opinions of experts point to the conclusion that the United States and all the signatories obligated themselves to a triple duty to work for human rights individually, in collaboration with other nations, and in cooperation with the United Nations.

An attempt in San Francisco to enact a bill of rights along with the charter failed. But the United States agreed with enthusiasm to the bold and sweeping vision of human rights set forth in the charter; Secretary of State Stettinius pledged that the United States would protect and promote the rights and freedoms enumerated in the charter.

In his closing address to the San Francisco UN Conference President Truman expressed these hopes and aspirations:

We have good reason to expect the framing of an international Bill of Rights acceptable to all the nations involved. That Bill of Rights will be as much a part of international life as our own Bill of Rights is a part of our

Constitution. The Charter is dedicated to the achievement and observance of human rights and fundamental freedoms. Unless we can attain those objectives for all men and women everywhere—without regard to race, language or religion—we cannot have permanent peace and security.

The United States Senate ratified the UN charter with only a handful of negative votes. That action, given the present climate of fear and suspicion about international commitments, seems astonishing. The legislative history of the ratification does not clearly indicate that the senators recognized fully the moral and legal revolutions that they were acknowledging and ratifying. The Senate furthermore did not make it clear whether or not the UN treaty should be self-executing, that is, whether the charter should become a rule of law binding upon a court without further legislation. The United States Constitution specifies that any ratified treaty becomes the "supreme law" of the land. The precise question of whether the UN charter has in fact become the "supreme law" of the land has never been presented to the United States Supreme Court. But in 1948 the Supreme Court in *Oyana v. California* struck down a California law that prevented American-born children of Japanese descent (whose Japanese parents were ineligible for naturalization) from owning land. The law, the Court ruled, violated the equal protection clause of the fourteenth Amendment. But four of the nine justices also held that the California statute, clearly inspired by anti-Japanese feelings, violated the obligations the United States had assumed by ratifying the UN charter. Justice Hugo Black, joined by Justice William Douglas, wrote that the California law violated the recently ratified UN charter. Justice Black asked, "How can this nation be faithful to this international pledge if state laws which bar land ownership and occupancy by aliens on account of race are permitted to be enforced?"

Justice Frank Murphy, joined by Justice Wiley Rutledge, echoed the same theme. He wrote that the United States had recently pledged itself to promote human rights through the UN charter and that "the alien land law stands as a barrier to the fulfillment of that national pledge. Its inconsistency with the Charter is but one more reason why the statute must be condemned."

If the decision of the nation's highest tribunal had gone the other way, the story of international human rights in America and the world might have been substantially different. The results in *Oyana* and other cases have been disappointing to human rights activists and scholars, who had hoped the Court would have found the charter to carry the full force of law binding in all jurisdictions. But efforts to change these results have not been successful. Virtually every court that has faced the question of whether the UN charter should be self-executing has backed away, asserting that it felt bound by the precedent in the *Oyana* decision. One can theorize, however, that if the UN charter had been ruled to be self-executing, the Equal Rights Amendment (ERA) might not have been deemed necessary, since the UN charter clearly bans discrimination based on sex.

But the fear that the courts might declare the sweeping guarantees of the UN charter to be self-executing prompted many jurists and organizations to endorse an amendment to the Constitution proposed by the late Republican Senator John Bricker (of Ohio). This proposal provided that no amendment to the Constitution would be self-executing and that no provision in any treaty would have any effect until both houses of Congress had made it a part of federal law. Although many legal experts felt that the Bricker Amendment set international law on its head, the amendment gained amazing support. Conservative and cautious people endorsed it because they did not want to be bound by the unexplored and even unknown provisions contained in the UN charter. Others influenced by the neo-isolationism of the 1950s and fearful of the implications of America's new foreign policy— the containment of communism—wanted to postpone any further commitments to the United Nations.

During the Eisenhower administration the State Department saw the revolutionary consequences of the Bricker Amendment and opposed it vigorously. The department argued that the executive branch of government had always been able to negotiate a treaty and, with ratification by a two-thirds majority of the Senate, make its provisions the "supreme law" of the land. Under the Bricker Amendment the ratification of an agreement negotiated by the White House would have no effect whatsoever unless, after the Senate ratified the treaty by a two-thirds vote, both houses of

Congress made it the law of the land by a simple majority vote. Spokespersons for the Eisenhower administration pointed out that this would alter something very fundamental in the separation of powers and make it almost impossible for any administration to guarantee to its allies that the provisions of a treaty beneficial to these allies would in fact be carried out once the treaty was ratified.

On February 26, 1954, the Bricker Amendment was defeated by a vote of thirty-one to sixty—by a one-vote margin, since a two-thirds vote was required. Unfortunately the amazing support for the Bricker Amendment expressed itself in other ways. The problem was complicated by the opposition to or confusion about the unanimous decision of the United States Supreme Court in *Brown v. the Board of Education* in 1954. Massive resistance to that historic decision developed immediately. Many Americans were not prepared intellectually or psychologically for the elimination of "separate but equal" public facilities. The argument was made that if the UN charter had been self-executing, the courts of America might already have banned schools segregated by race.

The controversy over the Court-mandated desegregation of schools clearly impeded any attention being given by the press and the public to United States participation in the development of the covenants derived from the UN Universal Declaration of Human Rights. In the turmoil of the 1950s hardly anyone ever mentioned the moral revolution engineered in large part by the United States as represented by the UN charter and the Universal Declaration of Human Rights. The Eisenhower administration, fearful that the Bricker Amendment would pass, promised the Senate that it would not move forward on the human rights covenants. And after the defeat of the Bricker Amendment the Eisenhower Administration never took the initiative in the area of international human rights.

The growth of the cold war in the 1950s and continued racial tensions in the 1960s discouraged almost all discussion of the role the United States should play in advancing international human rights. The struggle over Suez in 1957, the Cuban missile crisis in 1961, the turmoil over the civil rights law in 1964, and the war in Vietnam were only some of the events that deflected American concern from implementing the unprecedented promises made—largely because of America's moral leadership and creativity—in the UN charter. Looking back, it is both astonishing and disappointing that during those years the academics, the legal community, and the religious groups were so silent about the developments that should have been occurring in the United Nations with respect to human rights. Hardly anyone knew, for example, about the very successful European Court of Human Rights established in 1953 at Strasbourg by the twenty-five nations that make up the Council of Europe. Nor did many pay much attention to the work of the International Court of Justice at The Hague, the judicial arm of the United Nations.

It can be argued that an American foreign policy that increasingly emphasized containing communism precluded the United States from playing a major role in promoting human rights. Containment policy assumed that fundamental human rights were denied in Communist nations and that no improvement in that situation could be brought about by the United Nations or its specialized agencies. Containment policy also assumed that the United States should be the unquestioning friend and ally of all nations in the "free" world, overlooking the denial of human rights in authoritarian nations such as Guatemala or racist nations such as South Africa. The distinction between authoritarian and totalitarian regimes that became widely discussed in the early days of the Reagan administration was not a new concept. It had been accepted ever since America began its cold war policy of containing the Soviet Union. And in a very real sense it subordinated America's desire to see human rights guaranteed to its policy of bringing about restraints on Russia. The emergence of detente under Presidents Nixon and Carter was one of the many reasons why in the period between 1974 and 1980 the United States placed unprecedented emphasis on the observance of human rights. If detente continues to be set aside in favor of confrontation, this emphasis on human rights may also be diminished.

Whatever the reasons for the neglect by the United States of the full meaning of the UN charter, the fact remains that the charter is of immense significance. As the preamble states, it seeks to promote the rule of law by establishing "conditions under which justice and respect for the obligation arising from treaties and other sources of international law can be maintained." The charter also commits its signatories to "practice tolerance and live together in peace with one another as good neighbors."

It is commonplace today to speak of the limitations and failures of the United Nations. The global enthusiasm for that body in its early years is hard to discover now. That may be the fate of any institution destined, like the United States Supreme Court, to make difficult decisions. But even those who are most disillusioned with the United Nations seldom if ever urge its abolition. Its specialized agencies, such as UNICEF, the World Health Organization, and the Food and Agricultural Organization, are seldom criticized. But the sharp cutbacks in United States funds for the operational costs of the United Nations has brought great harm to the UN. One of the results of that cutback was the cancellation for the first time in history of the 1986 summer meeting in Geneva of the United Nations Commission on Human Rights.

THE UNIVERSAL DECLARATION OF HUMAN RIGHTS

The Commission on Human Rights, provided for in the UN charter and chaired by Mrs. Eleanor Roosevelt, completed its work rapidly and issued the Universal Declaration of Human Rights on December 10, 1948. That declaration articulates and expands on the major beliefs in the UN charter. It mandates that "every individual and every organ of society . . . shall strive by teaching and education to promote respect for human rights and freedoms." In an amazing proclamation Article 1 states: "All human beings are born free and equal in dignity and rights. They are endowed with reason and conscience and should act towards one another in a spirit of brotherhood."

In 1948 the United States was still a leader among advocates of human rights. In that year the then-Secretary of State George Marshall, opening the UN General Assembly in Paris, spoke of human rights in these terms:

Systematic and deliberate denials of basic human rights lie at the root of most of our troubles and threaten the work of the United Nations. It is not only fundamentally wrong that millions of men and women live in daily terror, subject to seizure, imprisonment and forced labor without just cause and without fair trial, but these wrongs have repercussions in the community of nations. Governments which systematically disregard the rights of their own people are not likely to respect the rights of other nations and other people and are likely to seek their objectives by coercion and force in the international field.

Although one could conclude that these moral sentiments derive from Western and Judeo-Christian values, the whole world has agreed to them. Do the followers of Islam, Hinduism, and Buddhism feel comfortable with the idea that all human beings "are endowed with reason and conscience"? Are they prepared to say that their relations with other nations should be conducted "in a spirit of brotherhood"? Non-Western peoples might perceive this document as reflecting a form of moral imperialism of the West. Perhaps the Universal Declaration of Human Rights is indeed an expression of global values on which there is consensus. But if this is so, does the declaration so dilute the values shared in common by all of humanity that it cannot really unite mankind on the crucial issues that divide the world?

And will Communist nations continue to adhere to the values of the declaration? Clearly the Soviet bloc does not comply with some of the guarantees of the declaration. These nations might eventually assert that they do not believe in the premises or the promises of the declaration, which has been called the most influential legal document in the history of the world. Clearly the Communist nations do not comply with Article 21, which states that "everyone has the right to take part in the government of [his or her] country, directly or through freely chosen representatives."

The sharp differences between the socialist and capitalist nations became painfully evident in the debate that continued for many years over the ranking to be given to economic and political rights. The hope in 1948 was that nations would adopt and ratify the thirty articles of the Universal Declaration of Human Rights and thereby make it the new Magna Carta of the world. But an impasse soon developed when the capitalist nations refused to agree to Article 23, which mandates that everyone has a "right to work," "to protection against unemployment," and "to equal pay for equal work." Even more difficult for nonsocialist countries was Article 25's demand that "everyone has the right to a standard of living adequate for the health and well-being of himself and his family"; these items include food, clothing, housing, medical care, and necessary social services. In 1948 the capitalist nations of the West were not about to commit themselves by treaty to propositions of this sweeping nature. The socialist nations, on the other hand, wanted to put into international law those economic objectives that were at the core of the commitments they had made to their citizens. Similarly the Third World nations emerging from the ashes of colonialism wanted international law to require all nations to guarantee the basic essentials of food, medical services, and social security.

The long stand-off between the capitalist nations and the alliance of socialist and developing countries delayed the adoption of the separate UN covenants on political and economic rights. Not until 1966 were these documents offered to the world for signature, and they did not enter into force until 1976. The economic and political rights now guaranteed by world law are therefore very new phenomena in the human family. We can only speculate how these unprecedented documents, pregnant with significance, will play out on the world stage. I am reminded of the adoption by the United States of the Thirteenth, Fourteenth, and Fifteenth amendments after the Civil War. It took many decades before the United States Supreme Court discovered the full thrust of the concepts in these amendments, such as equal protection under the law or due process. And the full implications of the seemingly never exhausted phrases of those amendments are still being discovered by federal and state courts all over America.

Will the political and economic covenants have a similar history? Will national courts begin to apply the guarantees set forth in these covenants? For example, efforts could be made to redistribute wealth so that the eighty-five million people in Bangladesh could receive additional economic resources or even be allowed to migrate to a nation where they can have those fundamental freedoms recognized by international law as the birthright of every human being. Such radical applications are implied in the language of the covenants.

The potential for the application and the elaboration of the commitments made in the political and economic covenants is staggering. It is easy, of course, to shrug them off and to declare them the work of dreamers. The covenants may be utopian, but they constitute promises that are now the patrimony of humankind. To be sure, the economic covenants do not even mention the labyrinthine problems that must be identified and resolved before some sort of social justice can be obtained for nations trying to leap in one or two generations from an almost primitive state to a modern industrialized society. But again, when governments or world society make solemn promises accepted and ratified by many nations, something enduring and immensely meaningful has happened.

Some treat the political and economic covenants with indifference, even disdain. They scoff at the idea that human rights could be protected by a global consensus or by a world tribunal. But the reality is that when nations want to advance their own selfish interests they find ways to cooperate. Mail is delivered in Moscow and Peking. Planes land in Iran and Ethiopia. Nations, however deep their animosities, agree on the definition of meters, tons, gallons, and microchips. New surgical techniques and novel forms of chemotherapy become known around the world almost instantaneously.

The acceptance of guarantees of basic human rights could one day come within the category of rights and agreements on which nations agree because not to agree would be contrary to their own selfish interests. Human rights could be described in a code as clear as the pharmacopoeia. Political rights such as the right not to be tortured or held without being charged could become as accepted and universally observed as the right of bankers and merchants not to be cheated by counterfeit money.

UNITED STATES RELUCTANCE TO RATIFY UNITED NATIONS COVENANTS

The flowering of the political and economic covenants has been immeasurably slowed by the failure of the United States Senate to ratify them. Although every major nation, including the USSR, has ratified these agreements and although they are now a part of international law, no president except Jimmy Carter has ever proposed their ratification by the United States Senate. The embarrassment and isolation that the nonratification by the United States brings to American Diplomats all over the world was painfully described by Charles Yost, ambassador to the United Nations during the Nixon administration, when he testified on November 14, 1979, before the United States Senate Foreign Relations Committee. This panel was considering the proposal by the Carter administration that the Senate ratify the covenants on economic and political rights.

Ambassador Yost urged the ratification of these treaties with these words:

> There are, in my judgment, few failures or omissions on our part which have done more to undermine American credibility internationally than this one. Whenever an American delegate at an international conference, or an American Ambassador making representations on behalf of our government, raises a question of human rights, as we have in these times many occasions to do, the response, public or private, is very likely to be this: If you attach so much importance to human rights, why have you not even ratified the United Nations conventions and covenants on this subject? Why have you not taken the steps necessary to enable you to sit upon and participate in the work of the United Nations Human Rights Commission? . . .
>
> Our refusal to join in the international implementation of the principles we so loudly and frequently proclaim cannot help but give the impression that we do not practice what we preach, that we have something to hide, that we are afraid to allow outsiders even to inquire whether we practice racial discrimination or violate other basic human rights. Yet, we constantly take it upon ourselves to denounce the Soviet Union, Cuba, Vietnam, Argentina, Chile, and many other states for violating these rights. We are in most instances quite right to do so, but we seriously undermine our own case when we resist joining in the international endeavor to enforce these rights, which we ourselves had so much to do with launching. . . .
>
> Many are therefore inclined to believe that our whole human rights policy is merely a cold war exercise or a display of self-righteousness directed against governments we dislike. We have spoken a great deal of the importance of our 'credibility' in connection with guarantees and assurances to allies. Here is a case where our credibility is very seriously questioned, but where we can reestablish it quickly by a simple act of ratification.

The testimony supporting Ambassador Yost's position was comprehensive and compelling. The 554-page record of the Senate hearings conducted in 1979 by the Foreign Relations Committee is a compendium of human rights law not duplicated in any other source. The Carter administration was determined to get the Senate finally to adopt four of the most important UN treaties on human rights. In a carefully crafted presentation Warren Christopher, deputy secretary of state, set forth the position of the Carter administration along with its reservations regarding specific provisions of the treaties deemed to be inconsistent or incompatible with American law. Nongovernmental organizations and human rights scholars joined in the testimony urging that ratification of four of the most important covenants promulgated by the United Nations and incorporated into international law would be of immense importance to the world community, to the credibility of the United States, and to the advancement of the human rights movement.

The reservations did not derogate in any essential way from the impact of the four covenants. The United States would not agree to abolish the death penalty. The Supreme Court decision in *Roe v. Wade* made it inappropriate to agree to the ban on abortion in the American Convention on Human Rights. And certain demands in the handling of those accused of crime could not be agreed to in advance, although the United States committed itself to move gradually to the adoption of the recommended practices.

The Carter administration made it clear that the covenants, if ratified, would not be self-executing. Consequently no provision in the four treaties would be binding on the United States unless Congress enacted a measure signed by the president making the provisions in the treaties a part of American law. Like the Bricker Amendment fought by Eisenhower, this concession, thought necessary to placate the Senate, was at odds with the Constitution, which categorically states that any treaty becomes the "supreme law" of the land.

The consideration by the Senate in February 1978 of America's first attempt at ratifying the human rights treaties was undoubtedly a milestone in the history of human rights legislation. Although the Senate never approved the recommendations of the Carter State Department, it is significant that an American president pushed so hard for ratification of these treaties. During both terms of the Reagan administration the State Department at no time ever proposed or apparently even considered a measure that would ratify treaties agreed to by every major nation in the world. Will another administration recommend what the Carter

White House did? Clearly it will happen if nonratification by the United States becomes a liability, a black mark, a sign of America's indifference to human rights. If the development of such sentiments is accompanied by demands for ratification by human rights advocates in America and around the world, the United States will, perhaps soon, drop its isolationism and agree that the guarantees made to mankind by the United Nations deserve ratification by the United States Senate. Until that time the United States will be perceived in the international community as a loner, victim of its own xenophobia, and a nation that, though formed by fifty-two million immigrants fleeing from oppression in other lands, has turned its back on those who live under authoritarian or totalitarian tyrannies.

The presidents who, from 1952 to 1978, made no recommendation to the Senate to ratify the major human rights treaties of the United Nations would not concede, of course, that their administrations were not carrying out a foreign policy in which the safeguarding of human rights was an important factor. The containment of communism, which became the centerpiece of American foreign policy in the 1950s, could be described as a program specifically designed to fight for the rights of those under the domination of the communists. The mission of the United States in this view of things would be as a full-time crusader for human rights.

But this does not fully explain why Presidents Eisenhower, Kennedy, Johnson, Nixon, and Ford never tried to fulfill the promises America made when the United States Senate ratified the UN charter in 1945. There are surely profound and probably shameful reasons for their silence. Why, moreover, was this silence broken by the Carter administration? Because of the growth of world opinion in favor of human rights or because of a deepening shame that America had abdicated the promises it made at the end of World War II?

The UN charter and the several seminal treaties that emerge from it form the matrix for the worldwide movement on behalf of human rights. That movement is still in its infancy. But even if international law can effectively proscribe the abuse of human rights, as it has in the cases of slavery and piracy, public and private groups devoted to human rights will still be needed because sovereign nations will still exist. And like most nations from the beginning of the era of nation-states, these nations will claim the right to restrict human rights in the name of national security or a state of emergency or any of the other multiple excuses devised by governments to silence or restrain their own citizens.

The work of protecting human rights, therefore, is a task that may never end. But the protection of those rights will be more easily carried out if 160 nations by education and enforcement promote observance of Articles 55 and 56 of the UN charter. The worldwide human rights movement will continue to extend its concern to the victims of the KGB, the political prisoners in Cuba, the displaced of El Salvador, and others who do not enjoy that decency and dignity which for the first time in the history of the world have become a part of the law of nations binding on the leaders of every nation in the world.

2. International Prohibitions against War Crimes, Racism, and Genocide

The number and range of human rights abuses now considered violations of international law is surprising, even astonishing. Because some observers may minimize the impact of this development, it is important to understand the extent to which human rights offenses have been interdicted at the highest possible level by covenants, conventions, treaties, and other international agreements. The terms *covenant, convention,* and *treaty* tend to be used interchangeably in international law. Though *convention* is often used for multilateral treaties of a law-making type, it is also used for various bilateral conventions, such as the consular conventions. *Covenant* was probably first used in an international law context by President Wilson in the Covenant of the League of Nations and has since been used for a variety of United Nations documents.

UN treaties, covenants, or conventions become international law in a three-step process. UN representatives of a country must sign the pact, the legislature of the nation must ratify it, and domestic legislation must be enacted to bring the nation into compliance. After these three steps have been completed a nation deposits an instrument with the UN secretary general attesting to its accession. According to Article 18 of the Vienna Convention on the Law of Treaties (1969)—a state that has signed a treaty subject to ratification must refrain from acts that would defeat the object and purpose of the treaty.

In addition to binding covenants, conventions, and treaties adopted by the General Assembly and ratified by the signatory states, there is customary international law. Defined generally as a common practice of a number of states that is required by or not inconsistent with established law, it has been difficult to apply.

The Universal Declaration of Human Rights, for example, was adopted as a resolution of the UN General Assembly. Although states that voted for its adoption did not bind themselves to adhere to its principles, it may be argued that it has become a part of the body of customary international law. Thus, while UN resolutions and declarations are not a formal source of law, they do reflect the common interests of the international community.

In recent years world law has internationalized offenses that have been under the jurisdiction of individual nations. International law has promulgated a humanitarian set of rules applicable to the conditions of war, banned racial discrimination in all its forms, and outlawed genocide, the deliberate killing of people because of their ethnic or racial origins.

THE CONDUCT OF WAR

It is ironic that warfare between nations was the first area to which the international law of human rights was applied. The origins of international laws regulating the conduct of war went through a process comparable to the contemporary evolution now transpiring with regard to political and economic rights. The preamble of The Hague Convention of 1907 mandated that belligerence "remain under the protection . . . of the principles of the law of nations, derived from the usages established among civilized peoples, from the laws of humanity and from the dictates of the public conscience."[1]

All the laws concerning the conduct of war were brought together and applied in 1946 at the Nuremberg trials. The United States and the USSR along with the Allied powers wanted to make it clear forever that there would be retribution against those who violated the laws of war and committed crimes against humanity—a term developed during the Nuremberg and Tokyo trials.

The Nuremberg trial condemned 21 of the top Nazi leaders. A second group of 185 lower-echelon defendants was also tried in the four zones of military occupation; 13 received the death penalty and 85 were imprisoned, 8 of them for life. The Nuremberg trials might well be characterized as the real beginning of international punishment for the violation of human rights; nothing like

Nuremberg had ever occurred in the history of legal institutions.

The Nuremberg Trials established that nations had the right and the authority to punish violators of human rights. It also established that a soldier may not be acquitted on the grounds that he was only following the orders of his superiors when he violated the rules of war. There are some evils, the Nuremberg tribunal concluded, that cannot be condoned or forgotten because they were committed in a war or because they were carried out by subordinates at the command of their superiors. That moral principle had not always been clear in the rules of war before World War II. The post–World War II Tokyo trials also established the principle of accountability for military commanders in the trial and conviction of General Yamashita. He was charged not with direct complicity in murders or the violations of human rights, but with negligence in allowing thousands of Japanese soldiers to violate the rights of the Filipino people, whose country the Japanese had occupied. The United States Supreme Court sustained that conviction despite the dissent of Justices Wiley Rutledge and Frank Murphy. The Nuremberg and Tokyo verdicts represent a victory for human rights on many counts. The one great tragedy is that neither the Allies nor the other nations of the world built upon these trials to create what jurists have written about for two generations—a standing international criminal commission, a sort of permanent Nuremberg.

The Nuremberg Principles were solemnly approved and ratified by the General Assembly of the United Nations in 1946. They were incorporated into the military law of England, the United States, and many other nations. Surprisingly these principles entered American law not by an act of Congress but by the decision of the United States Army. The army incorporated these principles into military law in its field manual of 1956, the Uniform Code of Military Justice.

The four Geneva conventions of 1949, to which the United States is a party, represent another significant attempt to protect war victims. The Geneva conventions make serious wrongs universally punishable but opt for punishment by each subscribing nation rather than by international tribunal. These documents oblige "each contracting party . . . to search for persons alleged to have committed, or to have ordered to be committed, . . .

grave offenses . . . and (to) bring such persons, regardless of their nationality, before its own courts." Article 4 of the General Provisions of the Geneva conventions extends the benefits of the conventions to persons who find themselves, "in case of a conflict or occupation, in the hands of a Party to the conflict or Occupying Power of which they are not nationals." Further, the benefits are limited to nationals of a state that is bound by the conventions. The Geneva conventions expressly prohibit violence to life and person, in particular torture, mutilations, or cruel treatment; the taking of hostages; deportations; outrages upon personal dignity, in particular humiliating or degrading treatment, or adverse treatment founded on difference of race, color, nationality, religion, beliefs, sex, birth, or social status; and the carrying out of executions without previous judgments by a regularly constituted court affording all the judicial guarantees recognized as indispensable by civilized peoples.

But in practice determining liability under the Nuremberg principles and the Geneva conventions remains difficult, precisely because nations are expected to judge themselves. The advanced technology of modern warfare has also created new moral dilemmas for which traditional principles cannot supply a precedent. The war in Vietnam, for example, tested Americans' determination to live up to its own military law and to those moral and legal principles formulated at the Nuremberg and Tokyo trials.

In the late 1960s lawyers and others in America began to urge that, regardless of what one thought about the merits of the war in Vietnam, it could not be won by the United States without massive violations of the laws of war. Those laws require that civilians in countries at war be treated with respect, that prisoners of war not be harmed, and that soldiers who violate these norms be punished. The very notion of "body count," vividly illustrated every night on the television news, seemed to be a violation of the rules of war set forth in the four Geneva conventions agreed to in 1949.

But until the news of the massacre of at least 128 Vietnamese civilians in the hamlet of My Lai on March 16, 1968, no violations had been prosecuted by the army. A cover-up followed, but the army, under intense pressure from Congress and the public, eventually charged twenty-five officers and enlisted men with My Lai-related offenses. In due course charges against nineteen of the twenty-five were dropped; two generals accused of participating in the cover-up received only letters of censure. Of the remaining six, all were eventually acquitted, except for Lt. William Calley, one of the platoon commanders at My Lai. He was indicted in September 1969 and convicted in March 1971 after a trial that brought into sharp focus America's failure to abide by the internationally recognized rules of war.

At his court-martial—the longest in history—Calley testified that he had never been told he was required to make a determination with respect to the legality or illegality of an order; he said, "I was never told that I had a choice." Calley stated that he and every American soldier in Vietnam had been instructed that all Vietnamese—men, women, and children—were potential enemies. Children, because they would not be suspected, were "even more dangerous."

Calley also referred to the pressure placed upon him by his superiors' insistence on a higher body count from his platoon. When Calley came to his company it had no body count, and he was told by Captain Medina to "try to catch up with everybody else." Lieutenant Calley stated that Captain Medina had "chewed me out a couple of times" when he failed to live up to Medina's orders promptly.

The jury in Calley's case knew that the entire world would be evaluating its verdict. Acquittal or a lenient sentence would in effect proclaim that the United States did not follow the rules of war accepted by all civilized nations or that the United States was so determined to win the war in Vietnam that it would somehow make those rules inapplicable. The jury deliberated for almost eighty hours, spread over thirteen days, before convicting Lieutenant Calley of multiple murders and sentenced him to life at hard labor.

The conviction brought forth a tidal wave of protests and of sympathy for Calley. The White House reported that in the five thousand messages it received the sentiment was one hundred to one for clemency. A Gallup poll revealed that 79 percent of the American people disapproved of the Calley verdict, only 9 percent approved, and 12 percent had no opinion. Dean Francis B. Sayre of the Washington Cathedral, writing in the *New York Times*, felt that the outcry for leniency came from "the lurking sense of sin that pervades our whole society over the war" and from the realization that "every one of us was tried and convicted in the Calley case."

Calley's appeals lasted for several years. After the Secretary of the Army reduced the sentence to ten years, Calley went to the federal courts. In 1974 a federal judge overturned the conviction on procedural grounds. In September 1975 the Fifth Circuit Court of Appeals reinstated the conviction, and on April 5, 1976, the United States Supreme Court denied review. The army then decided that Calley, having been confined for almost three-and-a-half years, should be released.

At the trial of Captain Medina, who was charged with three counts of murder and two of assault, the critical issue was whether Medina could be held accountable for the actions of his troops. The army field manual is clear on this issue. It makes the officer "responsible for acts of subordinates if he has actual knowledge or should have knowledge . . . that troops . . . subject to his control . . . have committed a war crime." The trial judge erroneously instructed the jury that actual knowledge was required. The prosecution strangely made no objection and Medina was acquitted on all charges. This acquittal seems inconsistent with the law set down by the United States Supreme Court in the case of General Yamashita, which specifies that a commander is liable for the crimes of his subordinates if he knew or should have known what they were doing and he failed to do what he could to prevent or punish them.

The review of the My Lai affair raises several troubling points. In convicting only Calley and in failing to prosecute anyone above the rank of colonel, the army apparently acted inconsistently. But a plausible case is made by the army that it did what it could in the cases brought to its attention, but the nature of the war made the application of the traditional rules of war very difficult. The army was also at a disadvantage in that soldiers were no longer chargeable with war crimes after they left the military. Because the My Lai incident brought into question the legality and morality of the entire conduct of the war, a nation torn by crises of conscience failed to pursue prosecution as fully as it might have.

If a Nuremberg trial—an international tribunal—were held to

judge the conduct of the military in the Vietnam War, it might clarify the moral complexities illustrated in the Calley court-martial. It would also raise the issue of whether America owes reparation for crimes against the Vietnamese people. When I was in Saigon in 1969 as a member of a human rights mission sponsored by the Fellowship of Reconciliation, I spoke to a Vietnamese lawyer. The lawyer pointed to hundreds of files in his office and explained that each file contained the evidence of atrocities committed by the United States military in Vietnam. He concluded his grim disclosures by suggesting that after the war the Vietnamese people would have their own Nuremberg and would convict many Americans—in absentia if necessary—of offenses he termed as bad, if not worse, than those for which Nazi and Japanese leaders were executed after World War II.

An international tribunal on the conduct of war would have ample cases before it today—the counter-revolution in Nicaragua and the questionable United States support for it, the war between Iran and Iraq, the Soviet invasion of Afghanistan, and the barbarism in Kampuchea. Ann and John Tusa's *Nuremberg Trial* (1983), a lengthy study of all that happened at the international military tribunal at Nuremberg, concludes on the sad note that although President Truman welcomed the recommendation of Attorney General Francis Biddle that the United Nations draft a code of international criminal law, that code has never been drafted. But the authors nonetheless point out that if nations decide to establish such a tribunal, they "would start with an advantage denied to those who set up the tribunal at Nuremberg. They would have a precedent."

RACISM

Just as clearly defined offenses against human rights committed during wartime violate world law, so too do activities based on invidious racist motivations. On December 21, 1965, the General Assembly of the United Nations unanimously adopted the International Convention on the Elimination of All Forms of Racial Discrimination. That covenant, which was born with the active support of the United States, has now become the most popular of all the treaties of the United Nations. It has been ratified by

129 nations, but not by the United States.

The covenant's language does not sound like the ordinary legal language of a treaty. It bristles with the anger and outrage of peoples who for decades have been treated as inferior because of their race or color. It infers that distinctions predicated on race are the result of "hatred." Here is some of the most explosive language ever used in any UN document: "Any doctrine of superiority or racial differentiation, is scientifically false, morally condemnable, socially unjust and dangerous."

Significantly all but a handful of the nations of the world have expressed their belief in a solemn covenant that states that racism is "scientifically false." Any theory that blacks are genetically inferior therefore has to contend with the condemnation of this idea in international law. The world has also concurred in the idea that racism is "dangerous." Equally striking, the signatories to the treaty expressed their alarm at "policies based on racial superiority *or hatred* such as the policies of apartheid, segregation or separation" (emphasis added).

This blunt identification of theories of racial superiority with hatred is perhaps the strongest condemnation of racism to be found in international law. The covenant forbids "all propaganda . . . based on ideas or theories of superiority of one race." In addition, states undertake to adopt "immediate and positive measures designed to eradicate all incitement to, or acts of, such discrimination." The treaty also requires that all signatories pledge themselves to make punishable by law "all dissemination of ideas based on racial superiority or hatred."

One of the most important features of the covenant on the elimination of all forms of racial discrimination is its authorization of affirmative action. It is virtually unknown that the practice of accelerating social integration, known in America as affirmative action, is authorized, indeed encouraged, by Article 1 of the covenant in these words:

Special measures taken for the sole purpose of securing adequate advancement of certain racial or ethnic groups or individuals requiring such protection as may be necessary in order to ensure such groups or individuals equal enjoyment or exercise of human rights and fundamental freedoms shall not be deemed racial discrimination, provided, however, that such measures do not, as a consequence, lead to the maintenance of separate rights for different racial groups and that they shall not be continued after the objectives for which they were taken had been achieved.

In Article 2 of the covenant the approval of affirmative action is specifically validated for action in the "social, economic, cultural or other fields." If the United States ratified this treaty, it would be bound by the provisions that allow, and possibly require, "special measures" to upgrade minorities who have been discriminated against. Even without ratification by the United States this treaty entered into force in 1969 and is now a part of international law. It is therefore arguably binding even on those who have not given final approval to it according to their own constitutional processes.

Significantly the Convention on the Elimination of All Forms of Discrimination Against Women, approved by the UN General Assembly by a vote of 130 to 0 with 10 abstentions on December 18, 1979, contains a similar provision authorizing "temporary special measures aimed at accelerating *de facto* equality between men and women." Such measures will not be considered to be discriminatory, but again they must be phased out as soon as they are no longer required.

The convention against racial discrimination provides for the establishment of a permanent committee of experts appointed by nations that have ratified the treaty. The United States, of course, has never had a delegate on that committee. An annual report to the General Assembly from the committee is required. There is now a right of petition by individuals who reside in nations that have ratified the treaty. Although the committee does not have the power to enforce its decrees or impose sanctions on those nations that violate them, its potential for promoting change is enormous. Through the mandatory submission of reports to the Committee on the Elimination of Racial Discrimination, nations party to the convention are subject to international scrutiny.

GENOCIDE

The very first treaty enacted by the United Nations condemned genocide. The Convention on the Prevention and Punishment of the Crime of Genocide was adopted on December 9,

1948, and entered into force on January 12, 1951. The treaty put into legal form a declaration made on December 11, 1946, by the United Nations General Assembly. This declaration rejected genocide as "a crime under international law, contrary to the spirit and aim of the United Nations and condemned by the civilized world." The convention defined genocide as killing members of a group with intent to destroy "a national, ethnical, racial or religious group." Included in this definition is the deliberate imposition on a group of "conditions of life calculated to bring about its physical destruction in whole or in part" and the establishment of "measures intended to prevent births within the group . . . or forcibly transferring children of the group to another group." Direct and public incitement to commit genocide is also forbidden by the convention.

Although most nations ratified this agreement shortly after its promulgation by the United Nations, the slow and tortuous process by which the United States Senate finally approved it in 1986 reveals a great deal about the ambivalence some Americans feel toward international treaties. The resistance to the genocide treaty in the United States Senate and by the American Bar Association up until 1976 typifies the tragic reluctance of the United States to consider itself as just another member of the family of nations. The fears or fantasies behind this reluctance are not always easy to analyze. They center on the feeling that Americans must not be exposed to the threat of being tried in a foreign nation. They also rest on the perceived, but not always openly acknowledged, belief that the amount of anti-American feeling in the world is rising and that Third World nations would like to use international legal machinery to satisfy political grudges against the United States.

The American Bar Association opposed the genocide treaty from the early 1950s until 1976, when it changed its position. Its opposition gave support to the extreme isolationists in the Senate and contributed a great deal to the long delay in ratification. From 1976 to 1986, due to an injection of new personnel at the ABA and a change in the climate of the country, the efforts of the American Bar Association were essential to the ratification of the genocide treaty, with reservations, on February 19, 1986, by a vote of eighty-three to eleven.

There is some hope that ratification of the genocide treaty by the United States Senate could finally lead to similar action on other treaties. But that hope will not be realized until there is an administration prepared to influence public opinion in favor of obtaining international guarantees for the rights that Americans receive from their own legal institutions. Americans suspect that international covenants guaranteeing human rights to everyone are only necessary for citizens in lands that do not partake of the freedoms Americans enjoy and that ratification of such treaties by Americans is not necessary and might be mischievous and dangerous.

Ratification of the genocide treaty might also break the Senate's long-standing resistance to giving its advice and consent to treaties negotiated by the White House. The Senate did ratify the Nuclear Test Ban Treaty in 1963 and the Antiballistic Missile Treaty contained in SALT I in 1972. But nuclear arms control pacts do not raise the spectre of American citizens being tried abroad, without right to jury, for alleged violations of human rights. Nor do agreements about nuclear weapons raise the possibilities that United States standards on civil rights, criminal procedure, or the role of women could be dictated from abroad.

3. United Nations Guarantees for Basic Human Rights

The ban by world law on war crimes, racism, and genocide is the most visible of the achievements of the United Nations human rights machinery. But the contributions of the United Nations and its agencies to the development of worldwide standards for human conduct range far beyond those three areas. Some of the two dozen United Nations treaties relate to specialized topics such as the nationality of married women, the status of stateless persons, or the treatment of refugees.

THE COVENANTS ON POLITICAL AND ECONOMIC RIGHTS

The central documents in the United Nations treasury are the International Covenant on Economic, Social, and Cultural Rights and the International Covenant on Civil and Political Rights. These two seminal documents sum up the aspirations of modern humankind. They were agreed to in 1966 by a wide variety of countries; a sufficient number of nations ratified the covenants so that in 1976 they became a part of customary international law. Although they only entered into force as a part of international law in 1976, their influence and impact are already profound.

The thirty-one articles of the International Covenant on Economic, Social, and Cultural Rights are grounded on the bedrock assertion in the preamble that "recognition of the inherent dignity and of the equal and inalienable rights of all members of the human family is the foundation of freedom, justice and peace in the world." Some of the thirty one articles are as revolutionary as the preamble. The frustration of newly emancipated colonies is echoed in the "right of self-determination" that "all peoples" are deemed to possess. In addition, again reflecting anti-colonialism, "in no case may a people be deprived of its own means of subsistence." Side by side with these broad ideas are the specific guarantees that all workers must receive "fair wages" and that women must be given "conditions of work not inferior to those enjoyed by men, with equal pay for equal work." Workers must also be guaranteed "periodic holidays with pay, as well as remuneration for public holidays." The document also recognizes "the rights of everyone to social security, including social insurance."

The treaty urges that "the widest possible protection and assistance should be accorded to the family, which is the natural and fundamental group unit of society." The family is further protected by the recognition of "the right of everyone to an adequate standard of living for himself and his family, including adequate food, clothing and housing and to the continuous improvement of living conditions." Those who wonder about the reality or feasibility of an international guarantee of a "continuous improvement of living conditions" will also raise questions about the requirement that "during a reasonable period before and after childbirth . . . working mothers should be accorded paid leave or leave with adequate social security benefits." This last guarantee has been commonplace in Europe for many years, but it is not yet firmly assured in any of the fifty states in America.

The rights to medical care and education are also guaranteed. Education, moreover, shall be directed "to the full development of the human personality and the sense of its dignity." The deep concern that almost every United Nations document expresses for human rights is reflected in the International Covenant on Economic, Social, and Cultural Rights, which demands that education "shall strengthen the respect for human rights and fundamental freedoms." Education shall also "promote understanding, tolerance and friendship among all racial, ethnic or religious groups."

While education should be compulsory and free at the primary level, "generally available" at the secondary level, and "equally accessible" at the college level, it should not be totally controlled by the state. In one of its least quoted provisions the covenant stipulates in Article 13 that all nations shall "undertake to have respect for the liberty of parents . . . to choose for their children schools, other than those established by the public authorities . . .

to ensure the religious and moral education of their children in conformity with their own convictions."

The fifty-three articles of the International Covenant on Civil and Political Rights, also adopted by the UN General Assembly December 19, 1966, parallel and extend the world vision clearly visible in the economic covenant. The rights protected are similar to what Americans call civil liberties. Everyone, for example, "shall have the right to freedom of thought, conscience and religion." That right "shall include freedom to have or to adopt a religion or belief of his choice, and freedom, either individually or in community with others and in public or private, to manifest his religion or belief in worship, observance, practice and teaching."

The mood of the world after World War II is again echoed in the political covenant. Article 20 states that "any propaganda for war shall be prohibited by law." And again the detestation of racism prompts the statement that "any advocacy of national, racial or religious hatred that constitutes incitement to discrimination, hostility or violence shall be prohibited by law."

In order to protect the freedoms guaranteed in the civil and political rights covenant a human rights committee made up of eighteen members was established. The committee will be available, however, only to those nations that voluntarily assent to the Optional Protocol to the International Covenant on Civil and Political Rights. Elaborate rules are set forth for the operation of the Human Rights Committee, which is designed to mediate differences and resolve disputes in the manner customarily followed by the many antidiscrimination agencies in the United States. The nations party to the political covenant are required to submit reports on the measures they have taken to promote the rights outlined in the covenant and to report on the progress made in the enjoyment of these rights. The Committee comments on the reports and submits its comments to the individual nations as well as to the Economic and Social Council. Nations party to the convention may also submit reports claiming that another nation is not fulfilling its requirements under the treaty. Extensive efforts are then made by the committee to negotiate an amicable solution on the basis of respect for human rights as recognized by the covenant.

THE CONVENTION ON ELIMINATING
DISCRIMINATION AGAINST WOMEN

The Charter of the United Nations was the first international treaty to spell out the principle of equality between men and women in specific terms. The UN charter requires all signatories to promote and encourage human rights and fundamental freedoms for all without distinction as to sex. The ban on discrimination based on gender is contained in several charter provisions and in the International Bill of Rights, the common name for the Universal Declaration of Human Rights, the International Covenant on Civil and Political Rights, and the Covenant on Economic, Social, and Cultural Rights.

The United Nations covenants were not the first to protect the rights of women. The Covenant of the League of Nations called for humane working conditions for all, irrespective of sex. The League's bylaws provided that "all positions within the League, including the Secretariat, shall be open equally to men and women." The International Labor Organization (ILO), established in 1919, has continually sought to ban discrimination against women in the workplace. In 1951 the ILO promulgated a convention requiring equal pay for equal work for men and women—a convention now in effect in over seventy nations. An impressive regional effort to protect women in Latin America has been directed since 1928 by the Inter-American Commission of Women.

The United Nations prohibition of discrimination based on sex was far ahead of the ban on gender bias enacted by the United States Congress in 1965. In 1945 Article 8 of the UN charter was adopted; it outlawed all "restrictions on the eligibility of men and women to participate in any capacity and under conditions of equality in its principal and subsidiary organs." In 1946 the UN Commission on the Status of Women was inaugurated. In 1952 the United Nations adopted the Convention on the Political Rights of Women, which outlaws all sex-based discrimination in all state-related functions.

But it was not until 1967 that the United Nations adopted a Declaration on the Elimination of All Forms of Discrimination against Women. Such declarations, more formal than recommendations, express the importance of the principle enunciated and the expectation that it will be ratified as an international convention. Twelve years later, on December 18, 1979, the United Nations finally adopted an International Convention on the Elimination of All Forms of Discrimination Against Women (CEDAW). This is the first international instrument to deal comprehensively with the condition of women and to establish standards binding on signatories. The convention entered into force on September 3, 1981, after ratification by twenty nations. As of September 1985 it had received ninety-three signatures and eighty ratifications. President Carter signed the covenant on December 17, 1980, as did several other heads of states in connection with the Copenhagen Conference on Women. The convention was sent to the United States Senate shortly after it was signed, but no action has been taken by that body.

The convention adopted in 1979 was to some extent the fruit of the International Women's Year in 1975 and the Decade for Women from 1975 to 1985. In 1985 the UN Commission on the Status of Women orchestrated worldwide events with the theme of integrating women in the work and development of the world. The UN Decade for Women culminated in Nairobi, Kenya, in July 1985, concluding the work started in Mexico City in 1975 and continued in Copenhagen in 1980. During those ten years there was undoubtedly more discussion about the rights and role of women than at any time since the establishment of the United Nations in 1945.

Although the treatment of women has been the subject of over twenty different international legal instruments since 1945, including conventions on the political rights of women, the nationality of married women, and the consent to marry, the International Convention on the Elimination of All Forms of Discrimination against Women is the first treaty to address a full range of issues related to the role and position of women in society.

One of the most important features of CEDAW is its elimination of most of the protective features of previous conventions. Protective action in some ILO documents totally excluded women from night work and mining. The perceived need was to protect a woman's health in view of her role as wife and mother. The authors of CEDAW resented and rejected laws that place women in a state of permanent inferiority or a subordinate status like that of children. Protective measures, however well intentioned, fortify the social definition of women as essentially familial and, rather than discriminate in favor of women, ultimately discriminate against them.

But there is one protective provision in CEDAW. Signatories are told that "special measures . . . aimed at protecting maternity shall not be considered discriminatory." Not all commentators are satisfied with this provision of unspecified "special measures." Could it lead to the exclusion of women from a wide variety of activities, especially during their childbearing years?

Another protective or corrective provision in CEDAW deals with the problems of rural women. This provision was inserted as a result of concerns expressed in Mexico at the 1975 UN conference celebrating International Women's Year. The convention spells out and vindicates the rights of women residing in "nonmonetized sectors of the economy" to have access to adequate health care facilities, to benefit directly from social security programs, to obtain "all types of training and education," and to have "equal treatment in land and agrarian reform as well as in land resettlement schemes."

Most of the thirty articles of the Convention on the Elimination of All Form of Discrimination Against Women set forth not protective or corrective measures but simple mandates forbidding discrimination on the basis of gender. Article 13 affords equality to women in bank loans, mortgages, and all forms of financial credit. Article 15 accords to women a legal capacity in civil matters identical to that of men. Women are given "equal rights to conclude contracts and to administer property" and equality "in all stages of procedure in courts and tribunals." In addition, men and women are granted "the same rights with regard to the law relating to the movement of persons and the freedom to choose their residence and domicile."

Although some of the rights contained in the Convention on the Elimination of All Forms of Discrimination Against Women had been treated in part in over twenty previous international documents, CEDAW is almost majestic in its comprehensive proclamation of the rights of women. It is the Magna Carta of all the global efforts to clarify and advance the status of women. It clearly moves beyond the customary or traditional definition of a woman as wife and mother. And it provides for its implementation by the formation of a twenty-three-member committee to advance the objectives of the convention in all appropriate ways.

American women and the United States government were very instrumental in the adoption of CEDAW in 1979. The adoption occurred at the height of the women's movement in America, during a period when the United States Supreme Court was strengthening the rights of women in American law. Although the Supreme Court has not yet held that distinctions based on sex or gender are inherently suspect, it has moved towards that position. But scholars watching the Court are generally of the opinion that the Court will not declare that discrimination based on sex violates the Fourteenth Amendment, which does not make reference to sex. In 1972 the Equal Rights Amendment was passed by two-thirds of both houses of Congress on March 22, 1972. But the Equal Rights Amendment obtained the approval of only thirty-five of the necessary thirty-eight states. Even an addition by the Congress of a period of several months to the customary seven-year period for ratification failed to produce the necessary votes by three-fourths of the states.

In the early 1980s the Equal Rights Amendment, reintroduced in Congress, failed to obtain the necessary two-thirds vote in the House of Representatives. If the ERA is not revived or ratified, would Senate ratification of the International Convention on the Elimination of All Forms of Discrimination Against Women produce the same result? If the convention were ratified as a treaty with no qualifications, it would, under the Constitution, be the "supreme law of the land." If it were ratified but categorized as not being self-executing, its provisions would not become law unless the House of Representatives and the Senate passed a bill and the President signed it.

It is a truism that the position of women in the world has changed more in the last four decades than in the previous four centuries. But long-held prejudices about the role of women in childbearing and childrearing, which were used to rationalize and justify the subordination of women, do not ordinarily evaporate in a short time. The global human rights revolution has been slow in embracing the rights of women and still has much to accomplish in this area.

4. International Efforts to Eradicate Torture

While the major human rights treaties are as clear and as definite as a document intended for world application can be, more particularized guidelines are needed by the 159 member nations of the united Nations. (A list of major human rights is provided in this volume.) There has not been adequate time for humanity to digest or even to assess the stream of human rights documents that has almost poured forth from the United Nations and other International groups. It is easy and commonplace to shrug off those treaties as ineffectual, but their potential impact should not be undervalued. Special attention is merited by the treaty on torture that was adopted by consensus by the United Nations General Assembly on Human Rights Day, December 10, 1984. Torture is condemned in international human rights statements more than any other offense against human dignity. The four Geneva conventions of 1949 forbid "cruel treatment and torture of persons taking no active part in the hostilities." They also proscribe attacks "upon personal dignity, in particular, humiliating and degrading treatment." It is also stipulated that "no moral or physical coercion may be exerted on a prisoner of war to induce him to admit himself guilty of the act of which he is accused." Both the European and American conventions on human rights forbid torture and degrading treatment. The African Charter on Human and Peoples' Rights adopted in 1981 includes "all forms of exploitation" within its condemnation of torture.

Torture has been forbidden by various UN documents, including the UN Universal Declaration of Human Rights (Article 5) and the International Covenant on Civil and Political Rights. (Article 7). The United Nations Standard Minimum Rules for the Treatment of Prisoners, agreed to by the General Assembly in 1957, ban corporal punishment and affirm that even for prisoners "all cruel, inhuman or degrading punishments shall be completely prohibited."

In 1979 the United Nations sought to prevent law enforcement officers from engaging in torture through the adoption of the Code of Conduct for Law Enforcement Officials. It ruled that they may "not inflict, instigate or tolerate . . . in human or degrading treatment or punishment." Nor may the orders of a superior or exceptional circumstances justify such conduct. In 1982 the United Nations, in its Principles of Medical Ethics, stated: "It is a gross contravention of medical ethics, as well as an offense under applicable international instruments, for health personnel, particularly physicians, to engage, actively or passively, in acts which constitute participation in, complicity in, incitement to or attempts to commit torture or other cruel, inhuman or degrading treatment or punishment."

Despite all these condemnations, torture has continued in an astonishing number of countries. Amnesty International estimated in 1984 that one-third of all nations were known to be engaging in torture for political reasons. As a result Amnesty International mounted a worldwide campaign to obtain the approval of the United Nations for a document that defines and prohibits torture.

The convention that won approval by the UN General Assembly on Human Rights Day, defines torture as

any act by which severe pain or suffering, whether physical or mental, is intentionally inflicted on a person for such purposes as obtaining for him or a third person information, punishing him for an act he or a third person has committed or is suspected of having committed, or intimidating or coercing him or a third person, or for any reason based on discrimination of any kind, when such pain or suffering is inflicted by or at the instigation of or with the consent or acquiescence of a public official or other person acting in an official capacity.

The ban on torture is absolute. Article 2 makes this clear by stating that "no exceptional circumstances whatsoever, whether a state of war or a threat of war, internal political stability or any other public emergency, may be invoked as a justification of torture." It is also stated clearly that "an order from a superior officer or a public authority may not be invoked as a justification of torture."

Over forty nations have signed the Convention against Torture and Other Cruel, Inhuman, or Degrading Treatment or Punishment, which has yet to be ratified by the requisite twenty states. These nations have agreed to enact "effective legislative, administrative, judicial or other measures" to prevent torture; have promised not to extradite a person to another state if that person would there be in danger of being subjected to torture; and have also agreed to educate their law enforcement personnel and all other individuals, such as physicians, who may come in contact with persons held in custody.

The convention against torture provides for a committee made up of experts chosen by the nations who ratified the agreement. The committee will be able to adjudicate claims of torture if all other remedies have been exhausted. Elaborate procedural safeguards and provisions for confidentiality are set forth in the conventions. In only one area was the convention against torture weakened. Article 20 empowers the Committee against Torture to investigate reliable reports of torture insofar as possible with the cooperation of the state concerned but with the right, even without that cooperation, to publish its findings after consultation with the nation concerned. This was the most controversial provision in the convention. In order to secure the convention's adoption Article 28 was added to permit countries to opt out of this provision, but such self-exclusion has to be done openly and explicitly.

Although the covenant against torture was agreed to by consensus, the first piece of international human rights legislation ever to be so adopted, it may take some time for it to become fully operational. The convention against torture will take effect when twenty nations have ratified it. The Committee against Torture will come into being when five countries have declared that they recognize its competence with regard to themselves.

The Reagan administration was supportive of the treaty against torture all through the drafting. Its UN representative joined the unanimous consent vote on December 10, 1984, but was not present on February 4, 1985, when the first twenty nations gathered to sign the convention. On Good Friday 1986 a group of church leaders sent President Reagan a letter urging him to sign the convention and submit it to the Senate for ratification. The sponsor of the letter, the Philadelphia-based American Christians for the Abolition of Torture, received a reply from the

State Department indicating that the United States intends to proceed toward ratification and full accession. A broad array of religious groups in the United States has urged the government to ratify the treaty against torture. Although United States citizens have never faced any serious problems with torture by their own government, they may still benefit directly from the convention against torture, which also prohibits actions that are "inhuman" or "degrading," a stronger standard even than provided in the Geneva conventions. These two terms are applied in the convention to both "treatment or punishment," thus conceivably bringing the death penalty and solitary confinement within the scope of prohibited actions.

The only major human rights treaty that the Reagan administration has recommended for ratification is the genocide pact. A similar initiative with respect to the convention against torture would be just as welcome around the world. Human rights scholars and activists in the United States fully expect that the White House and the State Department will urge the ratification of the convention against torture. But if the United States did urge the ratification of this convention without taking a position on the four major UN human rights treaties whose ratification was vigorously urged by the Carter White House, the hypocrisy of the United States would be apparent. Once again the United States, regardless of what it does or declines to do about the convention against torture, will appear as a laggard and even as a coward.

NONGOVERNMENTAL SANCTIONS AGAINST TORTURE

The adoption of the treaty against torture by the UN General Assembly was greeted worldwide with enthusiasm. The American Bar Association's House of Delegates in 1985 approved the proposed treaty and urged the White House to seek its ratification. Amnesty International is continuing its highly visible campaign to expose and eliminate torture. The momentum around the world seems likely to continue, especially in view of our increasing knowledge about the devastating impact of torture on the human psyche. In *Prisoner Without a Name, Cell Without a Number* Jacobo Timerman horrified the world by his description of what the military leaders of a civilized country, Argentina, did to secure the information its leaders desired. The indignities visited on Mr. Timerman, a respected journalist and editor of the daily *La Opinion,* are being inflicted on thousands of individuals in both totalitarian and authoritarian nations.

It is not possible to measure the relative seriousness of various types of human rights violations. Any denial of human rights, whether political, economic, or cultural, cries out for redress and restitution. But there is something particularly heinous about torture. This is an invasion of the soul of a person, a violation of a victim's personal integrity. It is an attempt to destroy a part of a person.

I heard firsthand of the insidiousness of torture when I talked at length with church-related human rights activists in Chile in 1984. These individuals operated a center that is both a clinic and a legal aid bureau for those who have been tortured by the Pinochet government. The psychological problems of the victims of torture are multiple. They know that if they continue their protest activities, they will be arrested and tortured again. Their fear of future torture collides directly with their convictions of conscience that they must continue to work for the return of democracy to Chile. Yet if they continue to risk arrest, can they be certain that they will not betray family and friends under torture? Will they end up with severe and irreversible psychiatric damage?

Those who in Santiago counsel the victims of torture have uncharted seas to explore. The victims have to live with themselves as long as tyranny in Chile exists. But they also have an obligation to balance the advantages of continued protest with the possibly permanent scars they will carry as a result of torture. Reflecting the growing concern over torture, some research centers have been established around the world to study torture and also the moral amnesia or psychological abnormality that afflicts those leaders who direct or carry out torture.

One of the by-products of the attention paid to torture by the United Nations and Amnesty International is the resulting mobilization of shame around the world. The World Medical Association in its Tokyo statement in 1975 made it unethical for any physicians to "countenance, condone or participate in" the practice of torture at the request of government officials. The Chilean Medical Association has carried out this mandate and made it clear that physicians who aid the government in any capacity in activities related to torture are likely to have their licenses revoked.

In 1975 the International Council of Nurses gave explicit guidelines for nurses paralleling the directives adopted by the World Medical Association. In 1977 the World Psychiatric Association in its Declaration of Hawaii called on psychiatrists "not (to) participate in compulsory psychiatric treatment in the absence of psychiatric illness."

In the 1984 trials in Argentina, as a result of which several top military officials were sentenced to jail for violations of human rights, the use of torture by government officials was fully exposed. As the world becomes more shocked and shamed at the use of torture, public officials everywhere may be more inhibited with respect to the use of torture.

If torture, already forbidden by law in at least 112 countries, becomes a violation of international law, would this eventually eliminate torture throughout the world? It might. Some might say that torture is an ancient, deep-seated evil, that the powerful will always use torture against those whom they perceive as a threat. But sunshine is a powerful disinfectant. It is especially powerful now that it is increasingly clear that a nation's reputation for justice and fair play is essential if that nation is to enjoy normal trade relations with other countries. Nations that employ psychiatric abuse against their own people, as the Soviet Union does, injure their reputation and their world standing in ways that become more apparent each day.

PUNISHING TORTURERS IN AMERICAN COURTS

An ingenious method to punish torture committed abroad was given by a 1980 decision of a federal court in New York. The Second Circuit Court of Appeals uncovered a statute enacted by the first Congress in 1789. Title XXVIII, United States Code 1350, grants to aliens a right to recover for civil wrong "committed in violation of the law of nations or a treaty of the United States."

In 1976 Joelito Filartiga, a seventeen-year-old youth, died under torture in Paraguay. As allowed by law, his parents brought action in Paraguay against his torturers, including Americo Pena-Irala, the inspector general of police of Asuncion. In 1983 a Paraguayan court of appeal upheld a ruling of the lower court acquitting the accused of the murder of Joelito.

In 1979 Pena-Irala was temporarily in New York, where he was arrested for overstaying his visa. Joelito's father and his sister Dolly brought action in New York for damages. Although the trial court declined to take jurisdiction, the appeals court in June 1980 ruled that, since torture violated international law, the plaintiffs could recover under the little-used provision of Section 1350 of Title 28 of the United States Code. For the first time in American jurisprudence a judge held that torture, when officially condoned, violates the law of nations.

In 1983 a judgment of $375,000 was handed down against Pena-Irala. Although that sum may not be collectible while the former public inspector remains outside the United States, the case against him led to a landmark decision. The words of the deciding judge are dramatic: "The torturer has become, like the pirate and the slave trader before him . . . an enemy of all mankind." The decision in *Filartiga v. Pena-Irala* implies that federal courts in America will assist foreigners present in the United States to recover damages against public officials in another nation who inflicted torture on them. Such a right of action is, however, surrounded by substantive procedural barriers. The defendant must be present in the United States and have assets here. The plaintiff must be able to produce witnesses to the fact that the torture took place and that damage resulted—daunting tasks in a nation far from the place where the alleged torture occurred.

Human rights enthusiasts in the United States and around the world were elated by the *Filartiga* decision. But its potential was possibly exaggerated. Its thrust was modified by a decision in the Court of Appeals of the District of Columbia in 1984. In that ruling *Tel-Oren v. Libyan Arab Republic)* a three-judge panel noted the lack of clear congressional guidance to ascertain the proper scope of the Alien Tort Claims Act.

Legislation to clarify the right of persons tortured abroad to recover damages in the United States has been filed in Congress. The proposed legislation would add a new dimension to human rights policy by serving notice to persons engaged in human rights violations that the United States will not shelter human rights violators from being held accountable in appropriate judicial proceedings in United States courts. The Torture Victims Protection Act, which authorizes compensatory and punitive damages, would authorize American courts to compensate victims of all those forms of torture condemned in a wide variety of international declarations.

If the United States enacted this legislation, would it substantially deter the practice of torture? The answer is clear from contemplating what would have been possible if such a legal procedure had been available to those victimized by President Anastasio Somoza in Nicaragua, President Ferdinand Marcos in the Philippines, or President Augusto Pinochet in Chile. The considerable United States assets of these repressive governments would have been available to torture victims who fled those nations.

It can be argued nonetheless that such a law might still have affected only a few cases. But a legal arrangement that authorizes the victims of torture to sue and recover in any nation could have considerable impact. It would mean that those who are chargeable as torturers or their accomplices would be reluctant to travel or acquire personal assets outside their own nations because they have damages assessed against them.

In October 1983 Amnesty International announced a twelve-point program for the prevention of torture. The program insists that all prisoners be brought before a judicial authority promptly after being taken into custody. States are requested never to allow confessions or other evidence obtained through torture to be invoked in legal proceedings. The training of law enforcement personnel is required and the ratification of the international treaties banning torture is urgently demanded. Point 10 of the Amnesty International program strongly recommends that the "victims of torture and their dependents should be entitled to obtain financial compensation." It is this last provision which might do more than any other reform to eliminate torture. Enactment of the Torture Prevention Act by the United States Congress would be an important, even a monumental step towards the abolition of torture.

It is very clear that torture is already a violation of the law of nations. Nongovernmental organizations have concentrated their anger and their labors on the eradication of torture. The contemporary activities of so many militant private individuals, government officials, and nongovernmental organizations is a phenomenon unprecedented in human history. It supports the hope that the history of torture, which can be traced unbroken from ancient Greece, may be finally coming to an end.

II. THE UNITED STATES AND THE HUMAN RIGHTS MOVEMENT

5. United States Reluctance to Ratify UN Human Rights Treaties

The United States, so influential in creating the UN, has failed to ratify the United Nations' central human rights documents. Particularly glaring is the failure, after concerted public pressure and political effort, to ratify the covenants on economic and political rights. These covenants have won the praise and admiration of virtually every American commentator. But they were statements to be admired rather than documents to be applied until President Carter proposed to the United States Senate on February 23, 1978, that they be ratified along with the International Convention on the Elimination of All Forms of Racial Discrimination and the American Convention on Human Rights. The failure of Carter's attempt highlights the roots of America's reluctance to commit itself to binding international agreements.

THE SENATE HEARINGS ON RATIFICATION

The Senate hearings on President Carter's proposal, conducted from November 14 to 19, 1979, attempted almost for the first time to make the adoption of the covenants a live option for America. The testimony was overwhelmingly favorable. The American Bar Association, the American Civil Liberties Union, the AFL-CIO, and the NAACP gave strong and unanimous support for ratification. The National Council of Churches (NCC), the United States Catholic Conference, and representatives of the Jewish community were lavish in their praise of these treaties.

Msgr. Frank Lally, testifying on behalf of the nation's 350 Catholic bishops, noted that in 1976 thirteen hundred representatives of dioceses and Catholic organizations, in a unique assembly to commemorate the bicentennial of the nation, urged the

National Conference of Catholic Bishops to ratify the UN covenants on civil and political rights and social and economic rights. Monsignor Lally did not take a position on all of the reservations outlined by the Carter administration, but he remarked that it was "a number exceeding that of any other ratifying state."

The bishops' testimony, presented by Monsignor Lally at the hearings, urged ratification "because we see in the substance of the rights enumerated in these treaties significant resonance with the enumeration of rights within the Catholic human rights tradition." The statement also expressed the bishops' support "because of our interest in strengthening the international consensus on this subject . . . [and] because of our interest in seeing the United States itself participate in the structures that have been established under these treaties."

Monsignor Lally testified that a policy urging ratification of the human rights treaties "stands solidly within the mainstream of Catholic social teaching, particularly as elaborated in Pope John XXIII's encyclical "Peace on Earth" and forcefully presented by Pope John Paul II in his address to the United Nations on October 3, 1979." It is noteworthy that Monsignor Lally attached the Pope's UN address to his testimony and requested that it be included in the record as supportive of the position of the United States Catholic hierarchy.

The National Council of Churches, with a membership of over forty million people from thirty-two Protestant, Episcopal, and Orthodox denominations, was as enthusiastic about the covenants as the spokesman for the Catholic community. The Reverend William L. Wipfler recalled the NCC's long and firm support of human rights treaties since the beginning of the new global consensus on human rights in 1945. Reverend Wipfler submitted twelve pages of testimony noting the close parallel between the policies of the NCC and those contained in the economic and political covenants. The similarities are striking. It is easy, indeed necessary, to conclude that the guarantees contained in the economic and political covenants of the United Nations are almost identical with the aspirations of the NCC over the past two generations. That same similarity with Catholic teaching is also very evident.

The Jewish community in America joined the Christian groups

seeking the ratification of the economic and political covenants. Speaking at the Senate hearings on behalf of the 107 councils and 11 national agencies that make up the National Jewish Community Relations Advisory Council, Sidney Liskofsky related that Jewish efforts to advance human rights in the modern world date back to attempts to have religious freedom included in the Treaty of Vienna. Mr. Liskosky recommended not only ratification of the covenants but also adoption of the Optional Protocol, which the Carter State Department had proposed deferring. Mr. Liskofsky felt that the Senate should accept the protocol and enable individual victims of human rights violations, after exhausting all available domestic remedies, to appeal to the UN Human Rights Committee established by Article 28 of the covenant. He also wanted the Senate to consider seriously the possibility of accepting the jurisdiction of the Inter-American Court of Human Rights based in Costa Rica.

The one opponent of ratification during the four long days of hearings was Phyllis Schlafly. Not claiming to represent any group, Mrs. Schlafly felt that the treaties would not "add a miniscule of benefit" to Americans and that they might well lead to the military conscription of women and to changes in American law related to women and the family. Mrs. Schlafly stated that "the treaties are incompatible with the United States Constitution." She asserted that they are "an exercise in folly, futility and frustration."

Senator Jessie Helms did not register any flat opposition to the ratification of the four treaties but made it clear that on the Senate floor he would insist that Article 17 of the nonbinding UN Declaration of Human Rights be included in the covenants. Article 17 states: "Everyone has the right to own property alone as well as in association with others. No one shall be arbitrarily deprived of his property." In the UN negotiations concerning the content of the economic and political covenants the socialist and capitalist nations obviously differed over the content and contours of the right to own property. The differences, which may have been irreconcilable, resulted in the absence of the item about private property in the two covenants that were finally agreed to in 1966. The Senate discussion on ratifying the treaties was not the place to consider reinstating an article on which the parties disagreed. A treaty contains all the points on which the contracting parties agreed. The Senate under the United States Constitution is required only to give its advice and consent. It is unclear whether some accommodation to Senator Helms' objection could have been worked out in the form of a reservation if the treaties had reached the floor of the Senate.

What is mystifying to students of human rights on the American scene and around the world is how all the energy and enthusiasm displayed in the Senate hearings on human rights in November 1979 could have evaporated or disappeared. The invasion of Afghanistan in the following month may have been one reason. That event may have altered America's perception of the Soviet Union although it had nothing to do legally or logically with the long-pending question of the ratification of the four most important treaties ever proposed by the United Nations. But the abrupt reappearance on center stage of the East-West rivalry somehow suggested to the Senate and perhaps to the nation that it was not an appropriate time to consider additional international commitments related to human rights. What is even more puzzling and saddening is that since 1979 there has been no serious attempt, either by the Senate or the White House, to try to do what every other democratic nation in the world has done—ratify the four major human rights treaties approved by the United Nations.

Will the United States ever try again to ratify the four most comprehensive and challenging affirmations of human freedom ever composed by the family of nations? It is pleasant to think that America will return to the path followed by all the major nations, but it is by no means certain. The United States could become even more fearful and frightened of international commitments, and to justify its rejection of the human rights covenants, it could reject the United Nations itself. It could do so not by a dramatic withdrawal from membership but by a gradual but significant cutback of appropriations for the United Nations. The justification offered would be the alleged domination of the United Nations by the Kremlin or the Third World or both. A virtual suspension of support by the United States for the United Nations could leave it understaffed and disorganized, a shell of what it is now and a ghost compared to the dreams the White House and the nation had for the United Nations when the United States ratified the UN treaty in 1945.

It is unlikely that politicians or political groups will be the prime movers in an attempt to reopen the issue of the ratification of human rights covenants. All too few constituencies will rally with enthusiasm to the political entity that makes a pledge to get America involved in complicated and mysterious agreements to guarantee the rights of millions of people in all types of countries around the globe. The role of the nongovernmental agencies is therefore crucial. They prevailed in San Francisco, where they were successful in making the promotion of human rights one of the top four objectives of the United Nations. The nongovernmental agencies, now growing in number and in strength, alone can bring the United States government back to the convictions that prompted the White House in 1979 to urge that the United States finally undertake the pilgrimage it pledged to follow in 1945 and 1948.

THE ROOTS OF AMERICAN RELUCTANCE

One of the strongest arguments that the NGOs offer for ratification of the human rights treaties is the need for additional protection for Americans' human rights. This argument, however, may be treated with scorn by many Americans who feel that they do not need any protection beyond the state and federal constitutional guarantees they now enjoy. Such a view, however, fails to take into account that for many decades of our existence as a nation the United States Supreme Court was wrong on fundamental issues related to equality for black Americans. Judicial error on this central question of justice for some twenty-eight million black Americans began with the tragic Dred Scott decision in 1857. The Thirteenth, Fourteenth, and Fifteenth amendments were passed to make black Americans equal before the law. But the Supreme Court again erred gravely. In 1883 it invalidated the civil rights measures enacted by Congress. In 1896 it failed again to give equality to blacks; in *Plessy v. Ferguson* it stated that separate but equal arrangements satisfied the United States Constitution. This unbelievable error remained the law of the land until the decision in *Brown v. Board of Education* in 1954.

If the United Nations human rights covenants had been in force during the period when the legal rights of blacks were being denied by the Supreme Court, this minority could have appealed to the international forum for relief. Similarly, if the United States Supreme Court should ever retreat to some form of tolerance of "separate but equal," the minorities of America could appeal to world law.

The possibility of Americans appealing for relief to world law or to an international court is an eventuality that arouses little enthusiasm in America. Americans are persuaded that somehow one of the three branches of government will always bring about a just solution to any difficult problem. But with all due respect to American government it is not true that some branch of the United States government has always resolved problems. For decades the United States Congress and many state legislatures were afflicted with antiquated and malapportioned electoral districts, so that citizens in urban areas were grossly underrepresented in state legislatures and in Congress. In *Baker v. Carr* in 1961 the Supreme Court finally asserted a constitutional right of all citizens to have roughly equal electoral districts so that one citizen, one vote, would be the norm in America. Similarly the country for decades allowed indigent people accused of serious crime to go unrepresented in court until the 1963 decision in *Gideon v. Wainwright*. Interracial marriage was forbidden in many states until *Loving v. Virginia* in 1967.

Would these changes have come about more rapidly and more effectively if there had been applicable international norms? The answer has to be yes. At least in the future international standards for human rights would strengthen and supplement the constitutional human rights standards now followed at the state and federal level in the United States.

The legal standards institutionalized in the economic and political covenants would be useful for another reason. Often in the United States there is no way to get any branch of government to reverse a denial of human rights made by another branch of government. Many issues are simply not reviewable by the courts or even by Congress. The Reagan White House, for example, refused to accept the decision of the World Court at The Hague asserting that the United States must pay damages to Nicaragua for the injuries done by the covert activity in the harbors of Nicaragua by the CIA or its agents. The United States vetoed this proposal when it was brought to the UN Security Council. There is no precedent for allowing a plaintiff to bring a lawsuit in federal or state court that would require this issue to be adjudicated. Nor can Congress force the State Department to reverse its decision and abide by the decree of the International Court of Justice (ICJ). But with ratification any administration or agency that disregarded the decision of the ICJ would also contravene the express intent of the Senate.

There are other untestable issues in American law and life. A litigant needs standing to sue and must demonstrate that he or she has been adversely affected by an arrangement that is challenged as unconstitutional. There are areas of cooperation between government and religion that in the eyes of many individuals are unconstitutional, but there is frequently no way to obtain a definitive resolution of this conflict. During the Vietnam War difficulty in establishing the right to sue prevented plaintiffs from being able to obtain a court order declaring that the White House and the Pentagon were acting unconstitutionally in prosecuting the war in Vietnam. The present mood against judicial activism is likely to continue and even to complicate further the capacity of aggrieved citizens to obtain judicial relief for what they perceive as a denial of human rights.

For reasons of self-interest the United States should therefore seek the ratification of at least the four major human rights treaties that were considered at length by the United States Senate in 1979. The indifference many Americans display towards the nation's legal and moral obligation to "promote" respect for human rights, as Articles 55 and 56 of the UN charter put it, derives from the combination of pride in American institutions, a fear of foreign involvement, a failure to comprehend the dreadful denial of human rights in so many nations, and a resistance to most "internationalist" ideas.

The indifference or hostility to making commitments to other nations was evident decades ago when the United States Senate rejected the League of Nations. The indifference almost disappeared when the Senate ratified the UN charter. But indifference regained ascendancy in a few years and is possibly stronger today than at any moment since the end of World War II.

The United States, like many other nations, is willing to abide by international law only when it suits American self-interest and interprets judgments counter to its interest as politically motivated and not binding. This jealous regard by a nation for its own sovereignty undermines the authority of international law—in particular the authority of the International Court of Justice.

The scorn for the United Nations of which the United States is capable reached a high point when the Reagan State Department refused to accept the jurisdiction of the United Nation's juridical arm—the International Court of Justice at The Hague. The United States during the Carter administration made effective use of the World Court when it pleaded there the case of the fifty-two hostages in Iran. The World Court made the unanimous judgment that Iran was in violation of international law. The United States sought to enforce this judgment in the Security Council of the United Nations only to be met by a veto from an unfriendly nation.

But when Nicaragua sued the United States in the International Court of Justice because of the complicity of the United States in the mining of the harbors of Nicaragua, State Department lawyers used every conceivable argument to complain that the International Court of Justice had exceeded its jurisdiction in considering a "political case" and that the United States was under no obligation to argue the merits of the matter. Additionally these lawyers contended that if the United States made its case, it would be required to disclose classified material related to military movements in Central America. The United States lost its case and, like Iran, registered a veto in the Security Council to terminate the litigation brought by Nicaragua with the aid of American lawyers. American lawyers protested this action vehemently and articulately. But no way has been found in the courts or in Congress to reverse a course of defiance of international law possibly unparalleled in American diplomatic history.

Can a nation that tramples upon the jurisdiction and role of the United Nations World Court be expected to ratify the principal treaties of the United Nations and thereby involve itself in additional commitments? Probably not, at least not at this moment in history. Most Americans respect their own tradition of adhering to the shining rational, constitutional, and humanitarian ideals at the heart of the American dream. Somehow one can hope that from this respect for democratic ideals a consensus will grow that it is inappropriate, inopportune, and indeed immoral for the United States to remain the only major democracy in the world to refuse to formalize its commitments to the United Nations by ratifying the major human rights treaties.

6. Commitments to Human Rights in United States Foreign Policy

Although over the last three decades the United States has been reluctant to enter into international agreements concerning human rights, its foreign policy has always exhibited a moral content. During this century America's political leaders have employed not a little high-minded rhetoric to explain and justify America's foreign policy. One could say that the policy of the containment of communism, which the United States has pursued since the early 1950s, is based on a commitment to use America's military might to prevent the takeover of nations that would become Communist and thereby violate human rights. Containment is predicated on the view that the United States in its foreign policy must pursue both America's interest and its ideals.

Before the United States Congress began a whole new series of initiatives in the area of human rights, the United States had always utilized moral issues as a part of its foreign policy. In reviewing that history it is difficult to make any accurate assessment of what impact, if any, the moral or human rights component of foreign policy decisions actually had. Were the human rights issues raised merely to make the utilitarian approach seem less crass? Was there really any meaningful component in the foreign policy decisions besides realpolitic? Or were the moral strains invoked by America's leaders a sincere attempt to have the United States serve its perceived moral objectives?

No overall answer seems attainable. But the presence of moral aspects in America's foreign policy is undeniable. Arthur Schlesinger, Jr., put it well in *Foreign Affairs* in 1978:

The United States was founded on the proclamation of single 'unalienable' rights, and human rights ever since have had a peculiar resonance in the American tradition. Nor was the application of this idea to foreign policy an innovation of the Carter administration. Americans have agreed since 1776 that the United States must be the beacon of human rights to an unregenerate world. The question has always been how America is to execute this mission.

The point has been made by writers from the far left to the far right that the United States cannot expect to prevail in the world if it is perceived to be offering only its own military power and a self-interested entrepreneurism. The point has also been repeatedly made that pragmatism and humanitarianism in foreign policy are not necessarily antithetical; nations and their citizens can be attracted by moral ideals as well as by pragmatic programs.

Many Americans feel that United States foreign policy is generally benign, humanitarian, and idealistic. And there is evidence to support this interpretation of America's dealings with other nations. The creation of the Marshall Plan, the establishment of the Peace Corps, and the billions donated through the Agency for International Development (AID) buttress the feeling that the United States has been a moral and humanitarian friend to many nations. Some could argue that these acts of generosity were performed in part for pragmatic and selfish reasons, the most prominent of which is the containment of communism.

Before 1974, however, congress issued few explicit statements as to what non-pragramtic elements should be contained in America's foreign policy. Enormous, almost unbridled, discretion was given to the executive branch of government in carrying out America's foreign policy. One of the few examples of an effort by Congress to identify and enhance the humanitarian dimensions of United States foreign policy is the Alliance for Progress program, which stipulated that a willingness to implement certain types of social reform was to be a primary criterion for the granting of United States economic assistance. Similarly the Foreign Assistance Act of 1962 directed the President, when furnishing aid, to "take into account . . . the extent to which the recipient country or area is showing a responsiveness to the vital economic, political and social concerns of its people and demonstrating a clear determination to take effective self-help measures."

In 1966 the Congress again attempted to incorporate human rights standards into the Foreign Assistance Act. The act stated that "in carrying out programs . . . emphasis shall be placed on assuring maximum participation in the task of economic development . . . through the encouragement of . . . local governmental initiatives."

In the 1967 version of the Foreign Assistance Act the president was directed to take into account "the extent to which the country is making economic, social and political reforms, such as tax collection improvements and changes in land tenure arrangements." But the motives with respect to Latin American nations were not entirely humanitarian or unselfish. Another criterion of the act was "the extent to which the country is creating a favorable climate for private enterprise and investment, both domestic *and foreign*" (emphasis added).

THE IMPACT OF SECTION 502B ON FOREIGN POLICY

It was not entirely unexpected or unprecedented for Congress in 1974 to initiate a bold program that required terminating all United States aid to those nations with dreadful human rights records. But in another sense the novel actions of a restless Congress introduced an entirely new dimension into the foreign policy of the United States. This dimension still awaits further definition and justification, and its durability as an *effective* policy is not entirely certain to all observers.

Congress had been moving in this direction for some time. In refusing to fund the war in Vietnam Congress expressed its revulsion at many of the hitherto well-established assumptions behind the doctrine of the containment of communism. Congress was also manifesting its embarrassment at America's identification with corrupt authoritarian regimes around the world. The scandals of Watergate also influenced Congress, at least indirectly. If the excesses of the executive branch of government could be checked by the enactment of several post-Watergate reforms, the executive branch could also be called to account by Congress for its support of foreign governments that systematically denied internationally recognized human rights.

The 1974 hearings conducted by the House Subcommittee on International Organizations and Movements, chaired by Democratic Congressman Donald Fraser of Minnesota, brought to light many instances of morally questionable foreign policy decisions.

The United States had extended military support to a Greek junta even after the junta was suspended by the Council of Europe; all of Greece's NATO allies save the United States adopted a policy of exclusion from the Council. When East Timor was occupied by Indonesian forces the United States did not join the clamor of criticism from United Nations member countries. The United States involvement in the coup in Chile in 1973 probably did more than any other event to bring about congressional insistence on foreign policy consistent with respect for human rights. Congress felt unable morally and psychologically to allow the United States to cut out virtually all assistance to the government of President Salvador Allende and then to provide abundant support to the military junta that came to power in a coup. This extraordinary series of hearings ended in a seminal report recommending that Congress and the White House place renewed emphasis on fulfilling the human rights aspirations of the UN charter.

The human rights legislation was part of the broad-based changes in foreign policy brought about by the Congress in the aftermath of the Vietnam War. The mood of Congress was very much in line with Professor Hans Morganthau's assessment of United States foreign policy:

With unfailing consistency we have since the end of World War II intervened on behalf of conservative and fascist repressions against revolution and radical reform. In an age when societies are in a revolutionary or prerevolutionary stage, we have become the foremost counter-revolutionary status quo power on earth. Such a policy can only lead to moral and political disaster.

The establishment of House and Senate committees that oversee the intelligence agencies, the enactment of legislation requiring that both Houses of Congress approve any significant sale of arms to foreign nations, the passage of the War Powers Resolution over the veto of President Nixon, and demands that executive agreements be submitted to the Senate for approval are some of the more visible initiatives of Congress. All these policies derived from a pervasive feelings that Congress had been bypassed in the formulation of foreign policy and that this course of action had resulted in the United States abandoning its ideals in favor of what was perceived by the White House, the State Department, and the Pentagon to be America's interest.

The congressional crusade for human rights that culminated in the passage of Section 502B of the 1974 Foreign Assistance Act was foreshadowed in 1973 with the adoption of Section 32 of the Foreign Assistance Act, which read, "It is the sense of Congress that the President should deny any economic or military assistance to the government of any foreign governments which practices the internment or imprisonment of that country's citizens for political purposes."

The text of Section 502B of the Foreign Assistance Act of 1974 contains stronger instructions on government action:

The President shall substantially reduce or terminate security assistance to any government which engages in a consistent pattern of gross violations of internationally recognized human rights, including torture or cruel, inhuman or degrading treatments; prolonged detention without charges; or the flagrant denials of the right to life, liberty and the security of the person.

The preamble to this mandate orders that the president

formulate and conduct international security assistance programs . . . in a manner which will promote and advance human rights and avoid identification of the United States, through such programs, with governments which deny to their people internationally recognized human rights and fundamental freedoms.

Congress also adopted a provision to this act placing a ceiling on military assistance to South Korea unless that nation made "substantial progress in the observance of internationally recognized standards of human rights." The same legislation called for a cutoff of military assistance to Chile and a limitation on economic assistance and prohibited the use of foreign aid money to train or support foreign police or internal intelligence forces. The year 1974 also saw the passage of the Jackson-Vanik amendment conditioning trade preferences for certain countries on their emigration policies. Democratic Senator Henry Jackson, of Washington and Democratic Congressman Charles Vanik of Ohio thus added the human rights component to the policy of detente.

In 1975 additional human rights provisions were adopted. Section 116 of the Foreign Assistance Act applied to all bilateral economic assistance. It converted the hortatory directives of Section 502B into a mandatory provision barring all foreign aid to nations that engage in a gross violation of human rights "unless such assistance will directly benefit the needy people in such country." That discretionary loophole remains in the law; little study has been done concerning instances where its employment might have subverted the intent of the ban on assistance to countries that violate human rights. In 1975 Democratic Congressman Tom Harkin of Iowa (now a senator) sponsored a successful effort to extend the human rights conditions to apply to aid to the Inter-American Development Bank and the Africa Development Bank.

The Nixon and Ford administrations fought the human rights initiative in Congress with some vigor. During his confirmation hearings in 1973 Secretary of State-designate Kissinger stated: "I believe it is dangerous for us to make the domestic policy of countries around the world a direct objective of American foreign policy . . . The protection of basic human rights is a very sensitive aspect of the domestic jurisdiction of governments."

In 1975 Secretary of State Kissinger refused to comply with the requirement that the State Department report on the extent of compliance by foreign nations with the conditions established by Section 502B. The report on compliance was prepared by the State Department but was never issued. In its stead Secretary Kissinger sent a message to Congress attacking the idea that decisions on military alliances with foreign nations should be linked to human rights. He stated bluntly:

Flagrant denials of human rights are not extraordinary events in the world community. . . . In view of the widespread nature of human rights violations in the world, we have found no adequately objective way to make distinctions of degree between nations. This fact leads us, therefore, to the conclusion that neither the United States security interests, nor the human rights cause would be properly served by the obloquy and impaired relations that would follow from determining gross violations.

In a corollary to this argument Secretary Kissinger claimed in 1976 that the Ford administration and the State Department objected to the legislation not because of its moral view, "which we share," but because legislation on such a sensitive issue was "almost always too inflexible, too public and heavy-handed a means to accomplish what it seeks."

In light of this resistance by the State Department the Congress in 1976 made Section 502B legally binding. The House report on this measure noted not only the failure to comply with the congressional mandate but also the State Department request for "increased levels of security assistance . . . for a number of countries where serious human rights problems exist." Section 502B was amended from a "sense of Congress" statement to a mandatory cutoff of aid. After President Ford vetoed a bill making the cutoff self-enforcing, Congress reenacted Section 502B, specifying a cutoff dependent on subsequent action by Congress.

Congress added to the law the following rationale for its policy:

> The United States shall, in accordance with its international obligations as set forth in the Charter of the United Nations and in keeping with the constitutional heritage and traditions of the United States, promote and encourage increased respect for human rights and fundamental freedoms throughout the world without distinction as to race, sex, language, or religion. Accordingly a principal goal of the foreign policy of the United States shall be to promote the increased observance of internationally recognized human rights by all countries.

The same section directs the president to formulate and operate programs of military aid in a way that will "avoid identification with governments which deny their people internationally recognized human rights." This language bluntly records the shame of Congress at seeing the United States linked to repressive regimes in nations such as Korea, the Philippines, Chile, and Argentina.

LIMITS ON THE EFFECTIVENESS OF SECTION 502B

In one sense the legislation on human rights that cleared Congress in the 1970s was very narrow. A nation could not be denied aid unless it engaged in a "consistent pattern of abuses." This language, borrowed from the civil rights legislation enacted in the 1960s, clearly excludes from condemnation a nation where abuses are not regular enough to constitute a "consistent pattern." A nation, moreover, must indulge in a "gross" abuse—thus excluding a wide range of delinquencies that could not singly or even collectively be termed "gross." The example of such offenses included in Section 502B makes it clear that the law is intended to apply to only those practices that are egregious denials of political (and not economic) rights.

The logistics of implementing the law have also been the cause of objections. American diplomats have protested the chore imposed on them by Section 502B—assessing the human rights record of the nation to which they are assigned. I have talked to ambassadors in Latin America who are professionally opposed to their imposed role as the source of information on the abuse of human rights in the country where they are sent to be a representative of goodwill, friendship, and harmony. There have been proposals for a United States Commission on Human Rights that would relieve the State Department of its duty under 502B of being the jury, the judge, and the decision maker regarding the termination of economic and military aid to various nations because of human rights violations.

But despite all the narrowing restrictions attached to Section 502B, the passage of this legislation is still of almost monumental importance. For the first time since the United States in 1945 solemnly agreed by treaty to abide by Articles 55 and 56 of the United Nations charter, Congress enacted a law designed to carry out America's "pledge" to "promote" human rights. Regardless of the effectiveness of the human rights legislation in the first years of its existence, the policy of the United States has been changed in a very basic way. By that legislation the United States agreed to monitor human rights in both totalitarian and authoritarian nations. The required annual State Department report on every nation's human rights record is a rebuke and a reminder that the United States finally and firmly is promoting those standards of human rights that it made a part of the United Nations charter and its legal machinery. If Section 502B had been enacted into law in the early 1950s, the foreign policy of the United States from 1955 to the present might have been very different.

The protection of human rights around the world would have been far more effective if the United States had worked through the United Nations and regional units for human rights rather than tackled the problem unilaterally through Section 502B. The legislation has created this anomalous situation: the nation that framed the human rights architecture of the United Nations but then refused to ratify the principal treaties of that organization now has created its own legal and political processes to make the

United Nations ideals of human rights applicable in the conduct of American foreign policy. History may reveal that the United States House of Representatives, where Section 502B originated, should have concentrated its zeal for human rights treaties. If the House had accomplished that objective, it would have made the United States a full and effective partner in the international struggle for human rights. Without such ratification the United States remains isolated, the only major nation to have walked away from the promises it made when the United Nations was born.

Section 502B even fails to make any reference to or use of the elaborate machinery of the United Nations for enforcing and enhancing human rights. Although the standards employed by and some of the language of Section 502B derive from United Nations practice, absolutely no reference is made to the UN Commission on Human Rights or any related organization of the United Nations. Nor is there any suggestion that the United States should collaborate with allies and friendly nations to improve the condition of human rights. The United States is to judge alone and to act alone. Section 502B is unilateral. It makes the United States alone the judge of the adequacy of another nation's compliance with internationally recognized human rights.

Many questions arise. Will the United States be charged with insincerity and a lack of faith in the very international institutions that without United States help could not have been formed? Will the judgments made by the State Department and Congress as they seek to implement Section 502B tend to supersede the decisions of the agencies of the United Nations? Or can it be argued on the other hand that the multiplication of tribunals to condemn the abuse of human rights is not undesirable since such courts add to global education and help to shame delinquent nations into compliance?

The initial enthusiasm for the enactment of Section 502B and its corollaries appears now to be less ardent, largely due to fears that the standards are not enforceable and are therefore of little value. But in the evaluation of any law the level of attainable compliance should not be the sole criterion; some laws are desirable even if it is difficult, even impossible, to bring about substantial compliance. No one is suggesting that the laws criminalizing rape, burglary, or the sale of narcotics be repealed even though the violations of these laws may be increasing. Similarly the gross abuse of internationally recognized human rights is so abominable that laws penalizing such abuse should be retained. If they present sometimes insuperable difficulties in enforcement, they nonetheless teach that certain deeds are evil and should have consequences adverse to the nation that sanctions or allows them. Constant reference to Section 502B when American foreign policy decisions are in question may sensitize the world to the primacy of human rights, thus making the United States a principal educator on the majesty and inviolability of human rights. One can argue that the attention given to human rights by Congress in the years 1974 to 1979 was one of the main reasons why the Carter administration in 1979 testified on behalf of the ratification of the major human rights treaties.

Section 502B and its companion measures were enacted because of the anxiety members of Congress experienced over the identification of the United States with authoritarian governments. The White House was told to stop doing favors for that kind of regime. Congress recognized that Section 502B would not give America the opportunity to penalize Communist countries, since the United States was not extending any aid to Warsaw Pact nations or to Communist countries such as China or Cuba. Hence Section 502B meant trouble for weak and relatively unimportant nations, especially those in Latin America. Nevertheless, Congress in the 1980s continued to approve what Congress did on behalf of human rights starting in 1974. It is very unlikely that Congress will repeal Section 502B even if a president were to request such action, which is unlikely.

The abiding presence of Section 502B as a part of America's foreign policy is a significant sign that the United States has sought to return to that devotion to human rights that it demonstrated during the formative years of the United Nations and that it retreated from when the Eisenhower administration declined to seek the ratification of the major UN human rights treaties. That abandonment of human rights has been corrected. The United States has again proclaimed its allegiance to the ideal of vindicating the human rights of every human being. The United States may still be delinquent in its devotion to the rule of law and the exaltation of human rights as these notions were conceived by the framers of the United Nations. But at least Congress ended a generation of silence and made commitments to the fulfillment of human rights that were never before a part of American law.

7. The Carter Administration and Human Rights

The first few weeks of the Carter administration saw a stress on human rights different from the emphasis any previous administration had given that topic. In his inaugural address President Carter signaled the leadership he would give in the area of human rights with these words: "Because we are free we can never be indifferent to the fate of freedom elsewhere. Our moral sense dictates a clear-cut preference for those societies which share with us an abiding respect of individual human rights . . . our commitment to human rights must be absolute." Just eight days after Carter's inauguration he received a letter from Andrei Sakharov, the Soviet nuclear physicist and dissident leader. The President responded to it, thus implicitly rebuking President Ford for refusing to meet with exiled Soviet author Aleksandr Solzhenitsyn and indicating by this gesture that his administration would seriously pursue its human rights goals.

On March 17, 1977, the new president told the United Nations something that no United States president had ever said before—that he would recommend the ratification of the major United Nations human rights treaties. The President reminded the country and the world that by agreeing to Articles 55 and 56 of the United Nations charter the United States and all other signatories pledged to "promote" human rights. The President openly proclaimed that "no member of the United Nations can claim that mistreatment of its citizens is solely its own business . . . all the signatories of the United Nations Charter have pledged themselves to observe and respect human rights."

Rejecting the Ford administration's concern that an emphasis on human rights might compromise national security, President Carter declared that a stress on human rights "should not block progress on other important matters affecting the security and well-being of our people and of world peace." He also noted in his UN address that "the provision of food, good health and education will independently contribute to advancing the human condition."

President Carter's credibility at the United Nations was strengthened by the fact that the young administration had already persuaded Congress to repeal the Byrd amendment, thus restoring a complete boycott on Rhodesian goods and bringing the United States back into compliance with the UN mandate the United States had defied for several years. The new president reaffirmed his commitment to human rights by pledging on April 14, 1977, in an address to the Organization of American States Permanent Council, that he would seek approval for the ratification of the American Convention on Human Rights.

The strong stress on human rights in the early days of the Carter administration was foreshadowed in the campaign when candidate Carter profitably employed the appealing theme of human rights. But the emphasis on human rights in the Carter administration was still new, striking, and somewhat unexpected. The issue was congenial to the new president; it harmonized with his religious faith and it was presumably to his political advantage to invoke human rights. He later acknowledged this advantage in his memoirs, *Keeping Faith*: "Judging from news articles and direct communications from the American people to me during the first few months of my administration, human rights had become the central theme of our foreign policy in the minds of the press and public. It seemed that a spark had been ignited and I had no inclination to douse the growing flames."

President Carter did try to present a balanced approach to human rights. In 1977, in an address affirming America's commitment to human rights, he added that "this does not mean that we can conduct our foreign policy by rigid moral maxims." He acknowledged that he fully understood the "limits of moral suasion" and that "we have no illusion that changes will come easily or soon." He felt that by enhancing human rights the United States would "regain the moral stature that we once had." He made note of the worldwide "preoccupation" with the subject of human rights and noted that no other country besides the United States was "as well qualified to set an example."

In June 1977 President Carter swore in Patricia Derian as the first assistant secretary of state for human rights and humanitarian affairs, creating a new bureaucracy to serve human rights. Secretary of State Cyrus Vance had already carefully articulated how the Carter State Department defined its role in advancing human rights. On April 30, 1977, at the University of Georgia Law School, Vance laid out the contours of a policy that would emphasize human rights more than that of any previous administration in American history had done. The secretary made it clear that "the advancement of human rights" was to be "a central part of our foreign policy." The rights to be protected were placed in three categories: the right to protection against violation of the integrity of the person; the right to food, shelter, health care, and education; and the right to enjoy civil and political liberties. Vance asserted that the United States would promote all these rights even though he admitted that there could be "disagreement on the priorities these rights deserve." Such a broad promise may have led to some complaints at a later time when it became clear that almost out of necessity the Carter State Department was required to direct its attention only to the first class of rights.

Secretary Vance foresaw the difficulties inherent in the unilateral enforcement by the United States of international human rights. Echoing President Carter, he promised that the State Department would avoid "a rigid, hubristic attempt to impose our values on others." He pledged the most careful fact finding before decisions were reached. He promised to steer away from the "self-righteous and the strident" in applying the means available, which ranged "from quiet diplomacy in its many forms through public pronouncements to withholding of assistance."

The secretary declared that "we place great weight on joining with others in the cause of human rights. The United Nations system is central to this cooperative endeavor." The secretary also acknowledged the importance of the ongoing Helsinki process, which came into being when thirty-five nations signed the Helsinki accords on August 1, 1975. Mr. Vance candidly admitted that "we are embarked on a long journey" but ended by reminding all Americans that "we always risk paying a serious price when we become identified with repression."

Congress, encouraged by President Carter's unprecedented commitment to human rights, acted to extend the range of human rights legislation. In 1977 Congressman Harkin and others moved to put restrictions on the participation of the United States in all international financial institutions (IFIs). The Carter administration, despite its strong advocacy for human rights, fought and defeated the Harkin amendment. After the House of Representatives voted to place rigid human rights restrictions on the participation of the United States in the IFIs, Senator Hubert Humphrey sought to moderate the measure in accord with the wishes of the State Department. But a rare mix of liberal, populist, and conservative votes campaigned for the United States to qualify its support of the IFIs on the grounds of human rights. Eventually Congress passed a compromise giving some latitude to the executive branch by not requiring that the United States veto the international loans. However, the administration was expected to use its "voice and vote" to advance respect for human rights in the international financial institutions.

Additional legislation passed in 1977 requiring the Export-Import Bank to "take into account . . . the observance of and respect for human rights" in the country for which a loan is authorized. In 1978 similar provisions were enacted by Congress to cover the Overseas Private Investment Act (OPIC). Comparable legislation was directed at the International Monetary Fund and the several international banks; all of these were required to seek to "establish human rights standards to be considered in connection with each application for assistance."

THE CARTER HUMAN RIGHTS POLICY IN OPERATION

The Bureau of Human Rights and Humanitarian Affairs established in 1977 within the State Department to carry out the purposes of Section 502B and related legislation cannot be faulted for inaction. Its annual report in March 1977 on human rights totaled 137 pages; its report in February 1981 came to 1,140 pages. Interagency working groups met diligently to define the problems, reconcile differences of viewpoint, and resolve difficult problems.

Although the withholding of aid from a few countries in Latin

America has received a great deal of attention and some criticism, it should be noted that actually there were relatively few countries for which there was any question of withholding aid. All Communist countries (the USSR, Warsaw Pact nations, Vietnam, Cambodia, and China) and the Soviet client states (Ethiopia, Afghanistan, Libya, Iran, Cuba, and South Yemen) are barred from receiving United States aid. Chile was denied aid by Congress; Pakistan after 1979 was barred under the terms of the Nuclear Non-Proliferation Act because of its pursuit of nuclear weapons capability; and South Africa was subject to an arms embargo because of America's adherence to a United Nations resolution.

Of the approximately seventy remaining nations, those in Western Europe, along with Australia, New Zealand, and Japan, had no serious human rights problems. Other nations such as Taiwan had blemished records on human rights but did not demonstrate "gross" abuses or a "consistent pattern" of human rights violations. The only nations left were the eight Latin American countries from which the Carter administration cut off aid and those nations in which the United States had sizable military installations, such as the Philippines, South Korea, Iran, and Zaire.

Was the Carter administration inconsistent in not terminating aid to the Philippines, South Korea, Iran, and Zaire? It should be noted that in enacting Section 502B Congress did not state that human rights should be the sole criterion for judging the merits of giving aid to nations. It did not, in other words, forbid reference to the military and strategic value of a nation to the United States. It also provided that under "extraordinary circumstances" the executive branch of government could give aid to a nation notwithstanding its unacceptable record on human rights. Presumably reasons of this nature permitted the Carter administration to allow aid to certain nations. Although the State Department never reveals the reasons for permitting aid despite the human rights record of a country, one can theorize that Zaire, being the source of nearly all the West's cobalt, a substance essential to the operation of high-performance jet engines, was made exempt from human rights scrutiny. Similarly Indonesia, a major supplier of oil, Iran, sharing a long border with the Soviet Union, and South Korea and the Philippines, having strategic importance to the United States, were left undisturbed despite their generally unfortunate human rights records.

The bare record of the number of nations denied aid does not, however, offer any real evaluation of the impact of the Carter administration's human rights policy in operation. The administration employed symbolism in creative ways and orchestrated a worldwide propaganda campaign in favor of human rights. By sending observers to the trials of dissidents in South Africa, Thailand, and the Soviet Union, the Carter administration made clear to the world that it cared deeply about human rights. By voting against more than fifty loans to some fifteen nations in the international financial institutions, the United States made clear the priority it attached to the observance of human rights. In 1978 the denial of twenty-three out of one thousand applications for export licenses after a review for human rights concerns again demonstrated the seriousness of the government.

Opposition to the human rights policies of the Carter administration was somewhat tentative and slow to emerge. There is some truth to the observation that the opposition did not crystalize until it became a part of the more generalized opposition to several features of the Carter administration.

In 1977 former Secretary of State Henry Kissinger, while realizing that the Carter White House policy ran contrary to that which he and the Ford administration pursued, graciously praised the administration. "I applaud and support this objective. The president has tapped a wellspring of American patriotism, idealism, unity and commitment which are vital to our country and to our time." In a seeming reversal of his former stance Kissinger also praised the program for human rights as constructive—"the world needs to know what this country stands for." He added that "human rights must be an essential component of our foreign policy."

Dr. Kissinger summed up his position in these words:

The accomplishment of the new administration is not that it originated the concern with human rights but that, free of the legacy of Vietnam and Watergate, it has seized the opportunity to endow the policy with a more explicit formulation. The aim of the Carter administration had been to give the American people, after the traumas of Vietnam and Watergate, a renewed sense of the basic decency of this country, so that they may continue to have the pride and self-confidence to remain actively involved in the world.

Kissinger did, however, warn of the dangers inherent in the new human rights policy, pointing out that if compromises were made for commercial or strategic reasons and sanctions were not imposed on nations important to the United States, it might turn out that "the weaker the nation and the less its importance on the international scene, the firmer and more uncompromising would be our human rights posture." Kissinger also warned that the provisions to cut off aid to nations with unsatisfactory records on human rights could lead to a new isolationism; the liberals would vote against aid to countries on the right, while conservatives would vote against help to nations on the left.

These warnings were phrased in a different way by Harvard professor Stanley Hoffman, writing in *Foreign Policy* in 1977. "The issue of human rights by definition breeds confrontation . . . it is a dangerous issue . . . the subject of human rights almost inevitably increases tensions with our enemies. If it is pursued very avidly, it diminishes the chances of cooperation on a number of other world order issues." Professor Hoffman also pointed out that any "human rights policy is . . . constantly complicated by the problem of consistency" and that "treating human rights separately from all other issues may distort foreign policy."

There was, however, little open opposition or even harsh criticism of America's new human rights policy. It filled a vacuum that was felt by everyone in the post-Vietnam era. People hoped with President Carter that the United States would "regain the moral stature we once had." At the same time not even the most ardent advocates of the new human rights policy were confident in 1977 that this idealistic program would work effectively. How it was supposed to work was not even certain. The State Department collaborated intensively with the assistant secretary for human rights and humanitarian affairs in seeking to consistently and logically apply the relevant congressional policies. Conferences and consultations multiplied within the State Department and the Defense Department. Career officials at the State Department and diplomats in friendly nations receiving United States aid sought valiantly for a decision in each individual case that would become a part of a coherent and understandable formula.

CHALLENGES TO CARTER'S POLICY

Argentina's protest against the policy of the Carter administration highlights the problems inherent in consistently applying human rights considerations to foreign affairs. Argentina protested in 1978 when the United States Export-Import Bank threatened to withhold a $270 million loan from Argentina because of human rights violations. A high official of Argentina pointedly asked why the Carter administration had not also suspended credits from the Export-Import Bank destined for Poland. Protests were also registered within the United States, where, allegedly, jobs would be lost because of the cancellation of the loan to Argentina. Open hostility to the human rights policy of the Carter administration and vigorous advocacy of the loan to Argentina was expressed by Ronald Reagan in his syndicated column in the *Miami News* on October 20, 1978. Since the article bespeaks open hostility to America's human rights policies and its author was to become president in 1980, it deserves reproduction here. It has a special meaning for me because I was one of the three authors of the Amnesty International report referred to by Mr. Reagan.

ARGENTINA'S VIEW ON HUMAN RIGHTS
BY RONALD REAGAN

There is an old Indian proverb: "Before I criticize a man, may I walk a mile in his moccasins." Patricia Derian and her minions at Mr. Carter's Human Rights office apparently have never heard of it. If they had, they might not be making such a mess of our relations with the planet's seventh largest country, Argentina, a nation with which we should be close friends.

No sooner had President Carter made his early and strong statement on human rights than born-again McGovernites began infesting various foreign policy-making levels, with an eye toward forcing any nation they could to tow the mark—and they defined the mark.

Nearly any charge made against the nations such as Argentina, Brazil and Chile was assumed to be true. Worse, the Carter Human Rights office has managed to hold up important sales to these and other nations.

Now comes a man whose moccasins Ms. Derian & Co. should try: Dr. Jose A. Martinez de Hoz, Argentina's minister of economy, came to the United States recently, and he put Argentina's story in perspective.

Martinez de Hoz is the architect of what may turn out to be one of the most remarkable economic recoveries in modern history. By March of 1976, Argentina's people were being crushed by a 920 percent inflation rate; and the government was falling toward chaos. Leftist terrorists worked day and night to tear the country apart. American businessmen were favorite targets of kidnappers. In Rosario, the U.S. consul was kidnapped and riddled with bullets.

The armed forces stepped in, as Martinez de Hoz explained, to bring continuity and to keep the country together.

Amnesty International estimated early last year that about 15,000 persons had disappeared under the new government. Martinez de Hoz said he thought the figure was "grossly exaggerated." He said that Argentina had faced a well-equipped, disciplined force of 15,000 terrorists who were "destroying the social fabric" of the country. "What the government had to do was to protect the human rights of 25 million people against a minority of people who had gone ideologically haywire," he said.

In this civil war atmosphere, "no quarter was asked and no quarter was given," he said. He did not deny that some innocents may have been caught up in the crossfire between leftist terrorists, right-wing vigilantes and government forces. Though the situation is virtually under control today, Martinez de Hoz says "it is a sad reality that there will be a certain number of people that the government will never be able to account for."

When this slight, quiet, Cambridge-educated man speaks about a return to democracy he speaks with a conviction.

Argentina's economic recovery shows every sign of making that day come sooner, not later. Inflation, though still sky-high by our standards, is down from that 920 percent to 102 percent. Tax collections have doubled, the deficieny has been systematically forced down almost to zero and no more printing press money is needed.

Ms. Derian, would you care to try on a new pair of moccasins?

It is not certain how widespread is the hostility to an American human rights policy as manifested in this article by Mr. Reagan. Reagan's premise apparently is that the military dictatorship of Argentina should be acceptable since it brought about law and order and that, furthermore, Argentina is an important nation "with which we should be friends." He opposes a supposedly realistic acceptance of the dictatorship's abuses to the Carter administration's human rights requirements as though realistic foreign policy were incompatible with advocacy for human rights. If these are the norms to be applied universally, the plea for insisting on the observance of human rights is indeed narrow.

Other critics of the Carter policy on human rights charge the policy could have been more effective if the United States had engaged its European and other allies in its "crusade" for human rights. If, for example, America had involved Argentina's major trading partners such as Japan, Great Britain, Germany and France, the likelihood of influencing the Argentine government would have been greater. It is uncertain, however, whether other countries, however devoted to democratic ideals and human rights they may be, would want to jeopardize their economic interests by advancing their ideals.

In an address in December 1978 President Carter demonstrated that he realized the existence and strength of the adverse reaction to his human rights policy. At an event commemorating the thirtieth anniversary of the Universal Declaration of Human Rights, Carter reiterated the need for the American government to respond to appalling violations of human rights. "The reports of Amnesty International, the International Commission of Jurists, the International League for Human Rights and many other nongovernmental organizations amply document the practices and conditions that destroy the lives and the spirit of countless human beings." President Carter indicated no retreat from the message of his administration: "The policies regarding human rights count very much in the character of our relations with other individual countries."

The President proclaimed his human rights policies a success with these words:

The effectiveness of our human rights policy is now an established fact. It has contributed to an atmosphere of change—sometimes disturbing— but which has encouraged progress in many ways and in many places. In some countries, political prisoners have been released by the hundreds, even thousands. In others the brutality of repression has been lessened. In still others there is a movement towards democratic institutions or the rule of law when these movements were not previously detectable.

But the President was apparently not persuaded that he had adequately defended his human rights policy against the rising number of people who were questioning its basic usefulness. He reinforced his case with these words:

Seldom do circumstances permit me or you to take actions that are wholly satisfactory to everyone. But I want to stress again that human rights are not peripheral to the foreign policy of the United States. Our human rights policy is not a decoration. It is not something we have adopted to polish up our image abroad or to put a fresh coat of moral paint on the discredited policies of the past.

The President concluded with a flourish: "Human rights is the soul of our foreign policy."

An editorial comment on this address, printed in the *New York Times* on December 8, 1978, chided the President for the lack of clarity in his human rights policy and for the lack of consistency in its application. But the editorial applauded the fact that after two years of the new policy at least the burden of proof now rested with those who wanted business as usual with "tyrants, racists and other enemies of democracy" rather than with those who sought foreign relations compatible with the ideals of the United States.

Assessments of the effects and the effectiveness of the human rights policies of the Carter administration will continue to appear. But as the first book-length evaluation, Sandy Vogelesang's *American Dream, Global Nightmare: The Dilemma of U.S. Human Rights Policy*, demonstrates, the answer depends on what norms are used for measurement. All these norms are elusive, but assuming the existence of some methods of measuring, for what do we search? Do we look to the enhancement of America's moral prestige, to the growth or decline of American trade, to the actual number of violations of human rights prevented or interrupted, or to a combination of all these elements? In the early days of the Reagan administration one heard a good deal about the alleged lapse of friendship between the United States and Brazil and Argentina during the previous administration. But there are few if any tangible signs that trade or military collaboration actually diminished because the White House sought an improvement in the human rights in these or other countries. The situation is comparable to those who complain that the 1977 Foreign Corrupt Practices Act, which forbids bribery by American corporate officials to obtain business abroad, is detrimental to American business overseas, although they have no empirical data to validate their allegation.

In *The Uncertain Crusade: Jimmy Carter and the Dilemmas of Hu-*

man Rights Policy, Joshua Muravchik reviews the four years of the Carter administration from a neoconservative point of view. Openly hostile to President Carter and some of the top officials in the State Department in the Carter years, he declares Carter's policy "a policy of national self-effacement" and states or insinuates that some of the highest officials in the Carter administration were naively unaware of the menace of communism. He points out and ridicules every conceivable inconsistency and ambiguity in the human rights policies of the Carter administration. He alleges that the Carter administration by "attempting to conduct a human rights policy that stood above ideology opted out of the very struggle for the idea of human rights."

But after pointing out several ways in which totalitarian nations are worse than authoritarian nations, Mr. Muravchik ends by praising the human rights initiatives of the Carter years. He cites with approval the statement made by the International League for Human Rights after Carter's first year in office: " 'Within the past year, human rights has for the first time become a subject of national policy debate in many countries. Human rights concerns have been the focus of discussion in international organizations and of greater attention in the world media. A most significant factor in this has been President Carter and the U.S. human rights policy.' " Mr. Muravchik agrees with Arthur Schlesinger's statement that that Carter campaign for human rights " 'for all its vulnerabilities . . . [has] placed human rights on the world's agenda—and on the world's conscience.' "

Finally, Mr. Muravchik expresses his conviction that President Carter is justified in claiming the following in his memoirs:

"The lifting of the human spirit, the revival of hope, the absence of fear, the release from prison, the end of torture, the reunion of the family, the newfound sense of human dignity—these are difficult to quantify, but I am certain that many people were able to experience them because the United States of America let it be known that we stood for freedom and justice for all people."

Those who have criticized the human rights dimension of the Carter foreign policy must recognize that to be both opposed in principle to the human rights innovations in United States foreign policy in 1974 to 1980 and also to be opposed to acceptance by the United States of those UN covenants that have now become a part of international law indicates a legal and juridical nihilism is hard to justify or even to comprehend.

Sometimes timidly, sometimes courageously, but always assiduously, the Carter State Department tried to fulfill the aspirations of the United Nations charter and the directives of the United States Congress. Human rights advocacy as a part of America's foreign policy now has a life of its own and may be impossible to suppress or obliterate.

8. The Reagan Administration and Human Rights

The human rights community in America and around the world knew that the election of Ronald Reagan in November 1980 would mean the derailing and even the destruction of much of what Congress and the Carter administration had done for human rights. There was no partisan or ideological support for the promotion of human rights in any of the groups that elected Ronald Reagan.

During the campaign Mr. Reagan associated himself with the attitudes of Jeane Kirkpatrick and her view that Carter's human rights policies were detrimental to the strategic interests of the United States. In the early days of the Reagan administration Secretary of State Alexander Haig and others made no secret of their intention to dismantle the human rights apparatus set up by Congress during the Carter years.

Human rights abuses increased in Haiti, South Korea, and El Salvador in the period between Reagan's election and his inauguration. Many in these nations and elsewhere thought that the human rights crusade of the United States was over. In South Korea over one thousand dissidents were arrested and sixty-seven opposition papers were closed. In El Salvador seven Americans were killed, including four American churchwomen. A group of seventy well-known United States clergy sent an open letter to the president-elect expressing the fear that "military governments in many countries are viewing your election as a green light" for human rights abuses. In South Africa the careful efforts of the United States and other leading Western countries to resolve the Namibia problem fell apart after the defeat of President Carter.

The transition team for the Reagan administration was hostile to human rights. The so-called Committee of Santa Fe, a group of conservatives promoting military resolutions to problems in Latin America, urged that the Carter emphasis on human rights be abandoned. In his first news conference Secretary of State Haig announced that "international terrorism will take the place of human rights in our concern because it is the ultimate of abuses in human rights."

The administration appeared to be in agreement with Jeane Kirkpatrick's distinction between totalitarian and authoritarian regimes. The new administration appeared to concur in her November 1979 statement in *Commentary* that the Carter human rights policy was ill-advised because it disregarded the "centrality" of the East-West conflict and revealed a "predilection for policies that violated the strategic and economic interests of the United States."

The actions of the Reagan administration were ominous. In the week after the election David Rockefeller of the Chase Manhattan Bank traveled to Panama, Chile, Paraguay, Argentina, and Brazil telling large audiences of businessmen that the new administration would set aside the emphasis on human rights that characterized the Carter years. In its first weeks in office the Reagan administration urged Congress to reinstitute military aid to Chile, Argentina, Guatemala, and Uruguay—all of which had been denied aid because of their records on human rights. At the same time United States representatives at the multilateral development banks were told to reverse the Carter administration's opposition to loans for right-wing governments in Latin America, South Korea, and the Philippines.

The formidable offensive the Reagan administration intended to mount against the human rights program of the Carter administration became clear in the nomination of Ernest Lefever for the position of assistant secretary of state for human rights and humanitarian affairs. Dr. Lefever stated on July 14, 1979, that "in my view, the United States should remove from the statute books all clauses that establish a human rights standard or condition that must be met by another sovereign government before our government transacts normal business with it, unless specifically waived by the President."

Under repeated questioning in the Senate Foreign Relations Committee hearings on his nomination, Dr. Lefever could only say that he "goofed" in this statement and that he now believed in Section 502B and related statutes.

Ironically the nomination that was designed to dismantle the entire human rights program initiated by Congress and implemented by President Carter highlighted it in a very dramatic way. The international human rights community found new friends and a much greater solidarity than anyone knew existed. The three days of hearings on Ernest Lefever were attended by overflowing crowds. The role of a relatively obscure bureaucracy in the State Department suddenly became a topic of national and international concern.

Along with other human rights activists I visited Mr. Lefever in the State Department office he hoped would be his. For three months he occupied it, had some input in policy, and, although unpaid, sought to direct all human rights work into the East-West conflict with which he seemed obsessed. It had never occurred to Dr. Lefever or to anyone else in the administration that the Senate would reject the nomination of a clergyman who had a Ph.D. in ethics from Yale. But in early June 1981, after nearly three weeks of debate, the Senate Foreign Relations Committee rejected Lefever's appointment by a vote of thirteen to four. Dr. Lefever's inconsistent statements before the committee and his eccentricities made it easier for the committee to reject Lefever. But even without these reservations the committee might have refused to confirm Lefever because the human rights work at the State Department had taken on a life of its own in the view of Congress and the country.

At the Lefever hearings one of the finest statements on behalf of the human rights program legislated by Congress was made by former federal judge Marvin E. Frankel, who spoke for the Lawyers Committee for Human Rights. "People everywhere know our claims. They are watching—they will continue to watch—how we live up to our promises. People who have now their freedom with our support will not forget what we did. People who suffered terror and bestiality while we stood aside will not forget either." Even more tellingly Judge Frankel concluded: "We have too often allowed the Soviets to set themselves up, falsely, as the champions of oppressed people. Dr. Lefever's policy would repeat and perpetuate that grave error."

The office of the assistant secretary for human rights was empty for four months after the defeat of Dr. Lefever. During this period the White House urged new loans to authoritarian governments in Latin America. UN Ambassador Kirkpatrick made visits to Argentina and Chile, where she refused to meet with human rights groups. But Congress and the press continually put the administration on the defensive. In late October 1981 a confidential memo allegedly authored by Elliott Abrams, then assistant secretary of state for international organizations, stated that "human rights is the core of our foreign policy." The memo, destined to start a new phase in the Reagan administration's approach to human rights, was greeted cautiously but gladly by the human rights community. The White House had given up on the hope of downgrading the issue; it now hoped to use it to supplement and strengthen its geopolitical crusade against communism. One of the key sentences in the memo asserted that "we will never maintain wide support for our foreign policy unless we can relate it to America's ideals and to the defense of freedom."

But the memo made no real commitment to the defense of human rights aside from the goal of containing communism. It endorsed human rights advocacy because this gave the government "the best opportunity to convey what is ultimately at issue in our contest with the Soviet bloc." A few days after the memo was circulated Elliott Abrams was nominated to be assistant secretary for human rights.

The memo (reprinted in the *New York Times* on November 5, 1981) had the approval of Secretary of State Haig and was obviously intended to resolve the desire of the new administration to eliminate human rights as a separate aspect of United States foreign policy with the political reality that such a phasing out was simply not possible. There appeared to be intrinsic contradictions in the document; while it pledged to carry out the law with respect to human rights, its principal premise was that "the difference between East and West is the crucial political distinction of our times." The accent on human rights was to be used to stave off the "movement towards neutralism in many parts of the world."

In effect, the memo redefined human rights issues in terms of the containment policy. The administration hoped to transform the bureau on human rights into an agency to carry out the overarching policy of the administration, which was formulated almost entirely in East-West terms. In a subtle rhetorical shift the memo urged that the State Department "move away from 'human rights' as a term and begin to speak of 'individual rights,' 'political rights' and 'civil liberties.'" But the pitched battle being waged outside the Reagan administration by a host of human rights advocates suggested to the author of the memo that "we can move on the name change at another time."

The memo, published just one year after the election of Reagan, expressed and tried to resolve the probably unresolvable position of those who desire to eliminate the burden Section 502B and related legislation placed on the State Department. There had been only modest Republican support for this legislation as it passed through Congress. There was no support for it in the Republican platform adopted in Detroit in 1980. And the cold war warriors chosen by Secretary of State Haig as his deputies sincerely did not see that the foreign policy of the United States had any place for a program of remonstrating with America's friends about their human rights records. Friends were friends because they were enemies of our enemies. If they engaged in abuse of their own people, the United States should go slow in rebuking them or stirring up dissidents or insurgents in a friendly country because this would only open up the way for the Marxists and the Communists to infiltrate and even take over.

Nor did Secretary Haig and his fellow ideologues think that the machinery set up by the United Nations for the adjudication of claims based on human rights was important for America. At no time did the Reagan administration ever state that it desired to ratify any of the major human rights treaties. The twin United Nations treaties on social and political rights entered into force in 1976 because nations from Communist, non-Communist, and nonaligned nations voted for their ratification. But for those who saw the East-West conflict as the only determining factor for United States foreign policy, the policy of advocating human rights on a nonpolitical, nonpartisan basis seemed politically irrelevant, if not dangerous.

With all its contradictions, inconsistencies, and ambiguities, the Abrams memo is characteristic of the Reagan administration's approach to human rights. One assumption is seldom absent: human rights are of value not by themselves but only if their attainment is consistent with and helpful to the containment of communism.

The Senate, weary of the controversies over human rights in the Reagan State Department, confirmed Elliott Abrams without great difficulty. Responding to tough questioning, he promised that the question of ratifying the United Nations treaties on human rights would receive his attention immediately after the reorganization of the bureau on human rights; as secretary Mr. Abrams never took a position on the advisability of ratifying those treaties.

CHALLENGES TO REAGAN'S HUMAN RIGHTS POLICY

With respect to its human rights policy the Reagan administration has been criticized for its lack of clear methods for carrying out its human rights policy, its reluctance to comply with or open defiance of congressionally mandated responsibilities in this area, and its insistence on subordinating human rights concerns to its immediate political goals. Assistant Secretary of State Elliott Abrams has tried to clarify some of the unresolved issues in administration policy. His foreword to the annual State Department report on human rights—required by Congress and issued each February—stressed political ideology and the containment of communism for the first time in the history of these reports. The report rebuked members of the United Nations Human Rights Commission for allowing human rights violations in the Soviet Union and Cuba to go "virtually unnoticed" while Latin American nations were "being singled out for condemnation." Mr. Abrams also took on the entire General Assembly of the United Nations, accusing it of following a double standard that "focuses on certain countries, almost ignoring the violation of human rights in Communist lands."

After these broadsides Mr. Abrams tried to define internationally recognized human rights in a way compatible with the East-West approach of the Reagan administration. He alleged that in the contemporary world there was "a real lack of consensus on these rights." He asserted that the Bureau on Human Rights and Humanitarian Affairs would seek to eradicate the causes rather than the effects of human rights abuses. How this was to be done was not clear. He claimed, without naming the legislation he was required by law to carry out, that there is "a fundamental consensus among the American people on the aims of human rights policy; there is disagreement only about means of carrying out these ends."

Throughout his tenure as assistant secretary Mr. Abrams adhered to this view. At a symposium on human rights in the Reagan administration, held at Georgetown University Law Center on March 22, 1983, Mr. Abrams put his thesis this way: "In a field as complicated as human rights, differences in policy are to be expected, and should be treated as legitimate intellectual differences rather than as fundamental moral disagreements."

Many in the human rights community challenge that distinction. They do not see institutional integrity in the way the Reagan State Department has carried out the law. These observers feel that the centrality of the anti-Communist feeling in the Reagan administration has blinded it to the evils inherent in the abuse of human rights when that abuse arises not from Communist motivation but only from the nonideological desire of a dictator to remain in power. Other observers would be less certain that the Reagan administration is "blind"—especially in view of the flexibility it showed when it became clear, as it did in the Philippines and in Haiti, that the tyrants were about to be ousted and that the United States should be associated with the successful insurgents.

It can be argued that the Reagan administration has followed human rights policies that violate the intent of Congress when it formulated laws binding on the White House. The first incarnation of Section 502B was intended to put the government on record as opposed to abuses of human rights not merely in Communist nations but more particularly in those nations with which the United States has friendly relations. Hence Section 502B was designed to broaden the generations-old policy of resisting communism by adding a positive, affirmative duty on the part of the United States to help those nations struggling against tyranny within and thereby assisting them in resisting the inroads of communism.

Although this Congress has been reluctant to make an all-out attack on the Reagan administration's approach to human rights, the Congress of a future administration may well conclude that the period of 1980 to 1987 was a detour, an elaborate evasion of what Congress intended when it enacted legislation making the protection of human rights an essential part of America's foreign policy. This Congress has, however, occasionally challenged the Reagan administration on human rights grounds.

A major challenge came when Congress demanded that before any additional aid could go to El Salvador, the president would have to certify that human rights abuses in that nation had been curtailed. In January 1982 President Reagan certified for the first time that the government in El Salvador was making a "concerted effort" to conform to international human rights standards. His remarks were greeted with open incredulity in the press. In "The Reagan Turnabout on Human Rights" (*Foreign Affairs*, summer 1986) Tamar Jacoby, deputy editor of the *New York Times* op ed page, described this certification as the moment when "open contempt and disregard for human rights issues" was "replaced by a hypocritical show of interest," since for the administration "human rights were clearly among the least important in a long list of concerns in El Salvador."

The President certified an improvement in human rights observance in El Salvador on two subsequent occasions and Secretary of State George Schultz certified an improvement for the fourth and last time in July 1983. Congress sent the money, but opposition to the war supported by the United States was expressed so vociferously—especially by the religious community—that in late 1983 the administration pressured the Salvadoran government to expedite the prosecution of those involved in the killing of the four American churchwomen in December 1980.

The long and contentious debate over El Salvador between the Reagan administration and the international human rights community centered on the crucial question, Can human rights in United States foreign policy be subordinated to the nation's larger geopolitical concerns? That is the underlying issue that fueled the acrimonious debate between Assistant Secretary Abrams and several human rights groups.

In a January 1985 report on the Administration's record for 1984 the Lawyers Committee for Human Rights, Americas Watch, and Helsinki Watch asserted that Assistant Secretary Abrams had "developed and articulated a human rights ideology which complements and justifies administration policies." In so doing, the report concluded, he had compromised his mandate and the integrity of the bureau for human rights. He had furthermore betrayed the cause of human rights by seeking to make these rights a matter of ideological policy rather than law. Assistant Secretary Abrams responded sharply to these charges. He attacked the objectivity of the members of monitoring groups, accusing them of being determined to do what they could "to restrain the American role in the world."

In the three years in which Mr. Abrams was assistant secretary for human rights he continuously reported that his office and the State Department were engaged in all kinds of "quiet diplomacy." Even the most militant of the human rights monitors are not opposed to the many forms of "quiet diplomacy"; the real issue is what a country should do when quiet diplomacy fails. History may record that Mr. Abrams had the thankless task of trying to use human rights as a mere tool of geopolitics. He was replaced by Richard Schifter, a soft-spoken diplomat not drawn to confrontation or controversy. The Reagan administration was finally able to quiet the clamor over human rights and to keep it out of the press. Human rights activists worry that the law is not being enforced and that the "pulpit" of the bureau for human rights is not being utilized as Congress intended.

THE ADMINISTRATION'S RECORD ON HUMAN RIGHTS

The insertion of political and ideological concepts into the area of human rights by the State Department under Assistant Secretary Abrams can be seen in a review of the years 1984 and 1985. During that period the Reagan administration denounced abuses in nations aligned with the Soviet Union or in countries considered hostile to the United States. Those denunciations, while deserved, would have been much more credible and effective if they had been part of an evenhanded effort to promote human rights worldwide. Clearly the one hundred nonaligned nations perceived the United States as using or exploiting human rights in order to pursue other agendas.

The Reagan administration's concentration on East-West tensions profoundly affects its positions on human rights. In 1984 Abrams sought to minimize political imprisonments and tortures in Turkey by emphasizing instead Turkey's geopolitical position—its shared border with the USSR. He also engaged in a personal assault on human rights activists concerned with Turkey by alleging that they were "ill-informed and self-righteous" and that they intended to "use this issue as a weapon with which to attack a vital member of the Western alliance."

In the same year the administration minimized abuses in other countries designated as allies. Secretary of State Schultz twice certified that the Duvalier government in Haiti was making democratic reforms when there was scant evidence of any progress in the area of human rights. President Reagan portrayed "a large Communist movement" as the only alternative to the Marcos dictatorship in the Philippines. Similarly in 1984 the Reagan administration portrayed President Zia of Pakistan as a battler for freedom in a troubled area of the world even though there was undeniable evidence that in Pakistan new laws authorized floggings, amputations, and stoning and that many political trials were held by military courts. In 1984 the administration downplayed abuses in Yugoslavia and the People's Republic of China, nations that were Communist but had some alliance with the United States.

The ceremony conducted at the White House on Human Rights Day, December 10, 1984, demonstrated visibly the essentially one-sided nature of the Reagan human rights policy. Of the twelve special foreign guests—victims of human rights abuses—none came from a nation aligned with the United States. No one was there to symbolize the brutalities that have occurred in places such as South Korea, El Salvador, the Philippines, or Guatemala. But there were victims present from the Soviet Union, Poland, Iran, Cuba, Nicaragua, Afghanistan, and Kampuchea.

Yet 1984 also saw some modest efforts to raise the issue of human rights abuses in friendly countries. President Reagan met with Bishop Desmond Tutu, and the White House began a gradual shift away from "constructive engagement" toward a more direct condemnation of apartheid. Secretary of State Schultz announced that he would raise human rights issues with the government of Indonesia during a visit to that nation. Assistant Secretary Abrams brought world attention to the gross abuses of human rights in Uganda. Continued United States pressure to reduce death-squad killings and disappearances in El Salvador brought some results. And in Paraguay, which had been under a dictatorship for more than a generation, the United States embassy sought to mitigate abuses.

In 1984 and 1985 the Reagan administration continued to resist compliance with human rights laws such as Section 502B. The White House was able to persuade Congress to acquiesce in its desire to eliminate a special reporting provision with regard to an improvement in human rights observance in El Salvador. Consequently it continued to send massive economic and military aid to that nation even though it would not be difficult to demonstrate that El Salvador was still engaged in a pattern of gross abuses of human rights. In 1985 the administration sought and received military aid for fiscal year 1986 for Guatemala, Korea, the Philippines, Pakistan, Turkey, and El Salvador even though the State Department's annual report documented the most serious human rights abuses in these countries. The administration has, however, respected the ban on military aid to Chile. The International Institution Act of 1977 contains a provision by which the president must certify significant improvements in human rights before United States military aid can be restored. Despite pressure to do so, the administration has not certified Chile.

In 1984 the Reagan administration continued its efforts to repeal Section 660 of the Foreign Assistance Act, which prohibits direct assistance to police or law enforcement personnel in other countries. That statute, first adopted in 1974, was prompted by widespread abuses committed by American-trained police units in countries such as Guatemala, Brazil, and Thailand. Its repeal was called for by Assistant Secretary Abrams in May 1984. Support for the repeal was found in the report of the National Bipartisan Commission on Central America chaired by Dr. Kissinger, which said that in some cases Section 660 had the "paradoxical effect" of "inhibiting our efforts to improve human rights performance." In 1985 the administration was particularly successful in obtaining the repeal of Section 660. Congress waived Section 660 to permit aid to police forces in El Salvador, Honduras, and Costa Rica. A request for $22 million for military and police aid in Central America was deferred by the Congress in 1985 and passed in compromised form in 1986.

The Reagan administration also maintained a policy of having United States representatives vote in favor of loans from multinational development banks to nations even if they were engaged in "a pattern of gross violations of internationally recognized human rights." Reversing previous United States policy, the Reagan administration has, since 1981, voted in favor of loans to Argentina, South Korea, Paraguay, Guatemala, the Philippines, Chile, and Uruguay. In 1984 the administration supported loans totaling more than $3 billion to at least nine countries where serious human rights abuses were occurring. The only loans the United States opposed on human rights grounds in 1984 were those to Uganda, Syria, South Yemen, and Angola. The Reagan policy of approving loans to Chile was reversed in 1986. But from 1981 to that time the Reagan administration supported fifteen loans, totalling $1.44 billion, to Chile.

The administration failed to fulfill its responsibilities under trade legislation, enacted in 1974, that granted preferential tariffs of billions of dollars to developing countries that sell goods to the United States, on the condition that these nations recognize the right of workers to organize and bargain collectively, to receive a minimum wage, and to work under acceptable working conditions. In 1985 goods from the Philippines, Haiti, Taiwan, Korea, and Zaire were deemed eligible for tariff preferences though it is not clear that these nations are in compliance with the human rights standards required by the law.

The Reagan administration has also made no effort to ratify the major human rights treaties. No pledges were made to ratify the following treaties: the International Convention on the Elimination of All Forms of Racial Discrimination, The American Convention on Human Rights, the International Covenant on Civil and Political Rights, and the International Covenant on Economic, Social, and Cultural Rights. However, during 1985 the administration did work on behalf of the genocide treaty—the only such international agreement it has favored. The genocide treaty, with several qualifications, some of them unnecessary and even harmful, was ratified by the Senate on February 19, 1986 by a vote of eighty-three to eleven.

The preoccupation with communism that has characterized the Reagan administration more than any administration since the cold war began has governed its policies toward Central America. The administration has pressed vigorously for $1.6 billion to prop up the government in El Salvador. It complied reluctantly with the certification procedure required by Congress—until it was eliminated by a presidential veto. The administration lobbied successfully for substantial military aid for the contras in Nicaragua even though the human rights record of this group of mercenaries is open to question. Reagan administration policies in Central America rest on the questionable premise that armies propped up by United States funding can prevent communism from coming to lands wracked by poverty and in desperate need of basic land reform. Clearly the human rights policies legislated a decade ago by Congress have had little applicability since 1981 to the tortured twenty-six million people in the five nations of Central America.

The militarization of Central America by the United States has resulted in the flight of many refugees to this country, and in this case the Reagan administration has been seriously deficient in complying with human rights law concerning refugees and persons seeking asylum in the United States. The emphasis on creating policy in terms of the East-West confrontation has again resulted in a program that favors refugees from Communist nations while denying refugee status to those fleeing from nations aligned with the United States. This policy has been especially brutal in its impact on persons fleeing Central American countries, especially El Salvador.

When Congress passed the Refugee Act of 1980 it defined a refugee as a person who has a "well-founded fear of being persecuted" on the basis of race, religion, nationality, political opinion, or social standing if returned to his or her own country. Congress sought to bring the definition of a refugee in American law into agreement with the standards of the United Nations. But the Reagan administration has selectively enforced this law. As a result in 1985, while 25 percent of all applications for political asylum were approved, only 3 percent of the Salvadoran applicants received asylum. In the same year 46 percent of the Soviets, 59 percent of the Rumanians, 73 percent of the Libyans, and 57 percent of the Czech applicants received asylum. In 1985 some 2,000 Africans were admitted; about 1,775 of those were from Communist-controlled Ethiopia and 75 were from Communist-dominated Angola. Only 138 refugees were admitted from all of Latin America; 135 of these were Cuban. These figures do not reflect the ideologically neutral criteria for admission contained in the Refugee Act of 1980.

The burden of the administration's one-sided interpretation of the Refugee Act of 1980 fell more gravely on immigrants from El Salvador than from any other nation. Thousands of Salvadorans have fled that nation since the United States in 1981 began sending massive amounts of money to the military-dominated government in El Salvador. Many of those persons have a well- founded fear of persecution if they return. Their plight has prompted the sanctuary movement, a program by which some two hundred churches receive refugees primarily from El Salvador and Guatemala and help to protect them against a government that seeks to send them back to their country of origin. The administration has prosecuted some of the leaders of the sanctuary movement. It has also opposed the Moakley-DeConcini bill, which would postpone the involuntary departure of immigrants from El Salvador until an investigation is made of that country's political situation or until hostilities there are terminated.

Criticism of the Reagan administration's approach to human rights has been extensive and severe. But almost everyone will concede that with some exceptions the administration has fulfilled the mandate of human rights legislation in its dealings with Poland, Rumania, and the USSR. Many, but not all, of the monitors of human rights would also hope that there has been a shift in thinking in the Reagan administration about human rights. The original hostility has been lessened. The president and the secretary of state have written and spoken with accuracy and dedication about human rights. And with respect to Chile and South Africa the administration has altered its position—due in part, no doubt, to pressure and political developments.

But one has to speculate as to what the state of human rights would be around the world if the Reagan administration had continued to advance the devotion of human rights that was so visible in the Carter years. Attitudes toward human rights within the

United States and around the world changed in the Carter years. Suddenly the United States was no longer looked upon as the giant that thought little about human rights. Although it is impossible to precisely measure the impact that change had on human rights conditions in countless countries, it is not fanciful to think that the awakening of Congress and the White House during the years 1974 to 1980 strengthened democracy in several Latin American nations and elsewhere.

III. HUMAN RIGHTS ADVOCACY AROUND THE WORLD

9. Regional Courts for Human Rights Violations

In the period after World War II there appeared to be a gap between international and domestic efforts to protect human rights. While the UN was addressing these issues on a global scale, national courts were constrained by local authorities. Regional courts emerged to supplement the role of the UN in meeting local concerns while remaining independent of any one nation's political ideology. In this chapter I want to examine how these courts operated in Europe, Latin America, and Africa.

THE EUROPEAN COURT ON HUMAN RIGHTS

After World War II England and France were major powers who participated in the Nuremberg trials. They obtained the veto power in the Security Council along with the United States, the Soviet Union, and China. They concurred with the initiatives of the United States in establishing human rights as one of the four principal objectives of the United Nations. They collaborated in setting up the UN Commission on Human Rights in 1948 and in incorporating the guarantees of the UN Universal Declaration of Human Rights into the covenants that finally became customary international law in 1976.

But England and France also gave support to the founding of the European Commission and Court on Human Rights at Strasbourg in 1953. It is not clear whether England and France would have concurred in this regional human rights agency if all the hopes for the enforcement of human rights at San Francisco in 1945 had been fulfilled within the structure of the United Nations. It may be that they felt that the newly acquired unity of the continent, as manifested in the Council of Europe and in certain unifying economic measures required by the Marshall Plan, would be reinforced by a human rights tribunal for the nineteen nations of Europe.

The European convention that established the court openly admits that the task of the commission and tribunal at Strasbourg is easier than the task of a comparable global agency would be because the European governments "are like-minded and have a common heritage of political traditions, ideals, freedoms and the rule of law."

Since its establishment in 1953 the European Court of Human Rights has issued some forty volumes of decisions. Never before in all of human history has a group of nations agreed to permit citizens to sue their own government in an international tribunal. To be sure, the grounds for jurisdiction and the subject matter of allowable controversies are carefully narrowed. But the process and the results are still amazing.

The European Convention for the Protection of Human Rights and Fundamental Freedoms is built on the philosophy of Locke and Rousseau and the general European tradition of stressing human rights—a tradition that culminated in the French Revolution. Based on that tradition the Netherlands, Belgium, Switzerland, Germany, Italy, and Austria developed in the early 1800s guarantees for human rights in their basic laws, although these rights were frequently referred to as social and political rights.

The decisions of the European court are applicable to the local law of the European nations in different ways. The national constitution or national court decisions make it impossible to directly apply the decisions reached at Strasbourg in these six countries: Iceland, Ireland, Norway, Denmark, Sweden, and Great Britain. In three nations—Austria, the Netherlands, and Luxembourg—the convention takes precedence over ordinary laws and even over subsequent laws. In the remaining countries the convention has the status of an ordinary law so that subsequent legislation can set it aside.

The convention makes it incumbent upon the contracting states to bring their law into conformity with the provisions of the convention. That includes the obligation to amend legislation to conform to the European convention except on those points on which a nation has expressed reservations. By reason of this provision Norway amended Article 2 of its constitution, which forbade Jesuits from settling in the country.

Challenges brought against various nations before the European court have prompted these countries to change their laws in order to avoid embarrassment. This has been done even though a nation's obligation to conform with a particular decision of the authorities in Strasbourg is not entirely settled. But the binding effect of a decision by the European court is confined to the individual case; the court at Strasbourg does not have the right to reverse the opinions of the highest courts of the member states, nor are these courts bound to follow the precedent set at Strasbourg. Despite these limitations the impact of the European court has been enormous. A 1983 book by Andrew Drzemczewski, entitled *The European Human Rights Convention in Domestic Law*, documents the amazing range of ways in which the European nations have accepted the results and the reasoning of the court at Strasbourg.

In some ways the European court reminds one of the United States Supreme Court before its decision in *Marbury v. Madison* in 1803. In that ruling the Supreme Court aggressively but adroitly asserted its right under the Constitution to declare an act of Congress unconstitutional. No such power to interpret is explicitly granted by the European convention, but as the Supreme Court did in the *Marbury v. Madison* decision, the court might choose to exercise such power. Article 8 of the European convention states that "everyone has the right to respect for his private and family life, his home and his correspondence." There is no mention of privacy in the United States Constitution, but the Supreme Court has established the right to privacy as an "emanation" from several guarantees in the Bill of Rights. It is quite possible therefore that the European Court of Human Rights, in its interpretation of the stated right to privacy in Article 8, will issue decisions that give privacy more protection in Europe than in all other regions of the world.

Article 9 of the European convention is also filled with potential for wide-ranging decisions. "Everyone has the right to freedom of thought, conscience and religion; this right includes freedom to change his religion or belief and freedom, either alone or in community with others and in public and in private, to manifest his religion or belief, in worship, teaching, practice and observance." Religious dissidents and believers in unpopular creeds will almost certainly find in Article 9 relief from any harassment or restrictions.

Other guarantees in the European convention are significant, even startling. There is a freedom to "impart information and ideas without interference by public authority and regardless of frontiers." Individuals are granted a right to "an effective remedy" when their rights are violated, even when "the violation has been committed by persons acting in an official capacity." The convention also forbids any discrimination on the basis of sex.

The European convention does not per se outlaw the death penalty. But its thrust is in that direction. There is now a treaty among European states to ban capital punishment, and that treaty influenced France's decision in 1981 to abolish the death penalty and send the guillotine to the museum. The treaty against the death penalty has been signed by fifteen nations and ratified by seven, including France.

However, the European commission and court are not revolutionizing the jurisprudence of a continent. The commission, which controls the essential threshold issue of the admissibility of applications by individuals, has been strict and parsimonious in granting review. Ninety percent of all petitions submitted are ruled inadmissible. In the cases granted review the commission has very wide powers of investigation. It can and does make on- site inspection of alleged incidents and has not been reluctant to make full use of this power. If the commission concludes that a nation has violated the European convention, aggressive mediation and conciliation are engaged in before the release of any report.

The bureaucracy also slows up the process at the European commission and court. It can take up to five years before all the elaborate proceedings are concluded. But despite all the shortcomings of the way in which the European convention has been implemented, it has produced an important, intriguing, and monumental body of case law on human rights in Europe.

England has been particularly affected by its involvement in the scheme to bring about a uniform system of internationally guaranteed rights in Europe. Great Britain, unlike most of the nations that belong to the European convention, has neither a written constitution nor judicial review of acts of Parliament. As a result many aggrieved persons in England, and especially prisoners, have petitioned Strasbourg for relief. One of the best-known cases in England involved a prisoner named Sidney Elmer Golder who had been sentenced to fifteen years for robbery with violence. From his jail cell on the Isle of Wight he sought to write to his member of Parliament complaining about what he conceived to be a violation of his rights. His letter was read by authorities and permission to forward it was denied. A letter to his lawyer was also held up.

Golder insisted that this action by penal officials violated Article 6 of the European convention, which stipulates that "everyone is entitled to a fair and public hearing within a reasonable time by an independent and impartial tribunal established by law." Golder pleaded that the charge of misconduct brought against him by a prison official entitled him to have access to his lawyer immediately.

Great Britain fought Golder's petition. Prison officials were particularly anxious that it be defeated. The ultimate decision vindicated Golder's position in part. In a decision of unbelievable length the European Court of Human Rights on February 21, 1975, held nine to three that Golder could not be prevented from contacting a solicitor. The court also held unanimously that Article 8 of the covenant, which, as noted above, gives the "right to respect for . . . correspondence," applies even to people in prison.

But the Golder decision had no direct impact on British practice. Even though the European court clearly held that England had violated Articles 6 and 8 of the European convention, the tribunal at Strasbourg had no power to compel England to comply with its rulings. Parliament is supreme and it has not acted to bring its practices into line with the decision reached in the Golder matter.

Rulings from Strasbourg on issues related to immigration and civil liberties have on several occasions embarrassed England. Civil libertarians in England have consequently stepped up their demands that England, following the example of Canada, adopt a constitution or, alternatively, accept the European Convention on Human Rights as the equivalent of a bill of rights for England. These are difficult issues for the people of Great Britain. They pride themselves on following the rule of law despite the absence of a written constitution. The question is further complicated by the fact that the call for some sort of judicial review would involve a judiciary made up largely of individuals chosen from the ranks of barristers, who traditionally have been very conservative.

Another case that made the European convention controversial in England involved a petition from Ireland against the United Kingdom for alleged torture of citizens in Northern Ireland. After conducting a lengthy series of hearings and hearing an enormous amount of evidence, the European Court of Human Rights ruled on December 13, 1977, that English officials had in fact tortured people held in detention in Belfast. The best lawyers in England were employed by the Crown in this case. They lost the case in a very lengthy opinion that by a vote of sixteen to one, held that the five techniques of torture employed by Great Britain "constituted a practice of inhuman and degrading treatment" in breach of Article 3 of the European convention. The decision was anticlimactic since months before the decision Great Britain had renounced the challenged practices of brutality and ill-treatment.

The decision on torture again highlighted the fact that of the nineteen signatories of the European Convention on Human Rights about two-thirds have made the rulings at Strasbourg legally enforceable and eighteen have other enforceable bills of rights. Britain alone has neither accepted the restraints of the European convention nor enacted its own bill of rights.

A less important decision involving Great Britain was the six-to-one ruling on April 28, 1978, by the European Court of Human Rights that held that the practice of whipping with a birch rod, or "birching," as punishment for a crime violated Article 3 of the European convention, which forbids "inhuman or degrading treatment or punishment." Great Britain felt a moral obligation to obey, since Article 53 of the convention states that "the high contracting parties undertake to abide by the decision of the Court in any case to which they are parties." In spite of this sense of obligation England did not comply; nonetheless, the decision at Strasbourg furnished encouraging publicity to those in England and around the world who are opposed to all forms of corporal punishment.

The importance or the impact of the European commission and court should not be exaggerated. One might suggest that it is only doing for Europe what the federal courts have been doing for the United States for almost two hundred years. But the jurists at Strasbourg who hammer out their decisions on difficult issues, complicated by delicate questions of jurisdiction, may be accomplishing more for the unity and the public morality of Western Europe than any other economic or political organization. In addition, the judges at Strasbourg are refining and articulating the content and contours of that canon of human rights that emerged in the UN Universal Declaration of Human Rights and in the twin covenants that followed from that declaration. Although the extensive literature on the European convention concludes that great improvements are possible and necessary, most observers would agree with A. H. Robertson, who in *Human Rights in Europe* noted that the "European system for the protection of human rights is the best yet established by any international organization."

THE INTER-AMERICAN COMMISSION ON HUMAN RIGHTS

Paradoxically Latin America, where some of the most shameful abuses of human rights have occurred, has come forward with the most comprehensive and compelling covenant on human rights ever proposed by any international body. Shortly after the adoption of the Charter of the Organization of American States in 1948, the American Declaration of the Rights and Duties of Man was adopted in Bogota in 1948, seven months before the adoption of the United Nations Universal Declaration of Human Rights by the General Assembly of the United Nations on December 10, 1948.

In 1959 the Inter-American Commission on Human Rights was established as one of the principal organs of the Organization of American States (OAS). The operating charter of the commission was approved by the council of the OAS on May 25, 1960, and its first meeting was held in that year. The commission receives complaints from individuals, organizations, and groups who allege violations of human rights in any of the OAS member states. The Commission then makes findings of fact and recommendations to redress the violations. In 1965, following United

States intervention in the Dominican Republic, the commission played a useful role in mediating differences between the two countries. In 1966 the OAS confirmed the power of the Inter-American Commission on Human Rights to consider individual complaints.

In May 1979, shortly after the American Convention on Human Rights entered into force, the Inter-American Court of Human Rights was established to protect and enforce the guarantees of the convention. In contrast to the commission on human rights, the court will not hear direct petitions from individuals nor will it hear a case until the commission or a state party to the convention acknowledges that the controversy cannot be settled by other means. Article 64 of the American convention also authorizes the Inter-American Court to render advisory opinions; this capacity in and of itself has almost incalculable potential.

Although the United States, as one of the twenty-nine signatories to the OAS treaty, participated in the development of the Inter-American Commission on Human Rights, it did not sign the convention until 1977. The convention has not been ratified by the United States Senate despite the Carter administration's request in 1979 that the Senate do so.

The Inter-American Commission on Human Rights was created to "develop an awareness of human rights among the peoples of America" and "to make recommendations to the governments of member states . . . for the adoption of progressive measures in favor of human rights." It is also mandated to prepare studies and reports on human rights and to request information from all Latin American nations in matters of human rights.

Although the Inter-American Commission on Human Rights, based in San Jose, Costa Rica, is an agency little known to the general public, it is a daily working companion to the nongovernmental agencies like Americas Watch and the Washington Office on Latin America that report on and represent individuals whose human rights are violated. These groups exploit the implications of the 82 articles of the American convention. They seek to take advantage, for example, of Article 44, which allows the commission to consider petitions lodged by persons or NGOs without the consent of the government involved. This is in contrast to Article

25 of the European convention or Article 14 of the Convention on the Elimination of All Forms of Racial Discrimination, which stipulate that a petition may be filed only if the state against which it is brought has consented to be thus challenged.

The American convention is the most ambitious and far-reaching document on human rights even elaborated by any international body; its unique features include its prohibition of abortion, its banning of the death penalty, and its requirement of special criminal proceedings for minors.

In certain cases the convention also authorizes compensation for the victims of human rights offenses. Although the United States Senate would have to ratify this provision expressly, it poses the embarrassing possibility of Latin American individuals and governments suing American citizens or the United States government in the court in San Jose or in other tribunals. Despite its professed devotion to the rule of law and to the advancement of internationally recognized human rights, the United States has been reluctant to take the final steps to ensure the success of the American convention and the protection of human rights in Latin America.

It may be too soon to assess the impact of the relatively new legal machinery for human rights in Latin America. It is an infant as international agencies go. It is groping to find its way. The literature about it tends to be authored by lawyers who are bothered by all the arcane mysteries of the jurisdiction or the esoteric puzzles of the procedures to be followed by the commission and the court.

The most visible decision of the Inter-American Court on Human Rights has been its ruling in 1986 that no Latin American nation may license journalists. Such a procedure, the court ruled, violates the broad guarantees in the American convention for freedom of speech and press.

The commission's regular reports on the state of human rights in all the Latin American countries and its thoroughly documented studies on repression in individual nations clearly have been helpful in changing the climate of opinion in Latin America. The reports of the commission have been praised for their candor, detail, and balance and as superior to comparable reports from other official bodies. But governments are unlikely to credit international human rights groups for the advancement of human rights in their own countries. They are more apt to claim that the state of emergency is no longer necessary or the cause for some questionable imprisonment has been resolved. It is thus difficult and impolitic for the Inter-American Commission on Human Rights to claim victory. In addition, there has been in Latin America (as there is elsewhere) a gentlemen's agreement among governments to overlook each other's atrocities.

The work of the commission and court will at least obstruct any retreat to the old days when each sovereign nation was treated as if nothing it did to its citizens, no matter how monstrous, would subject it to inquiries by any international body. The commission in Costa Rica, while it neither deploys nor proposes sanctions, proclaims to a continent that it will establish facts about the denial of human rights, that it will prosecute in appropriate cases, and that it will abide by its mandate to proclaim the good news that liberation from the abuse of human rights is available to the 400 million people of Latin America.

There has been an almost dazzling shift away from military governments in Latin America since 1980. Argentina, Bolivia, Brazil, Ecuador, El Salvador, Guatemala, Honduras, Panama, Peru, and Uruguay have all moved to some form of civilian rule. The Inter-American commission and court would be hesitant to claim credit for this extraordinary movement, but history may record that one of the causes for this resurgence of democracy was the moral power of the American Convention on Human Rights and the legal power of the first human rights tribunal in Latin American history.

That the United States has had no significant role in the development of the Inter-American commission makes the proclamations of the United States on behalf of human rights in Latin America sound rather hollow and hypocritical. If the United States ratified the American convention and became involved in the work of the new agency in Costa Rica, the results could not help but be momentous. The "colossus of the north" would finally be another sovereign nation sharing its aspirations for human rights with twenty-eight other equally sovereign nations. The United States would almost certainly be required to yield on some issues. America might be embarrassed. There would be a new forum in which the nations of Latin American could protest what the White House and Pentagon are doing in Central America. There would be harangues against Yankee imperialism, denunciations of United States multinational corporations, and a repetition of the Third World rhetoric that has been heard so often in the United Nations General Assembly. But there would also be a new juridical method to bring the grievances of Latin America to adjudication and resolution. In articulating and advancing the rule of law the jurists in Costa Rica will be relying on a profoundly sound definition of law uttered by an unknown commentator: Law is made up of "those wise restraints which make men free."

THE AFRICAN CHARTER ON HUMAN AND PEOPLES' RIGHTS

In 1981 at the eighteenth summit meeting of the Organization of African Unity (OAU) the leaders of the fifty-one member states adopted the African Charter on Human and Peoples' Rights. By this act Africa joined Europe and Latin America in creating its own regional organ for the protection and promotion of human rights.

The human rights movement in Africa has been developing since at least 1961. After the fall of some of the cruelest dictators in Africa, including Idi Amin, Senegal submitted a resolution to the OAU in 1979 urging the establishment of some juridical organization to replicate what was being done in Europe and Latin America. The proposed document was accepted by consensus in July 1981. The charter will enter into force three months after the majority (twenty-six) of the OAU states have deposited their instruments of ratification with the OAU in Addis Ababa.

The African charter on human rights reiterates the basic principles of the charter the OAU agreed to in 1963. The need for decolonization and the elimination of apartheid are the top priorities. Similar importance is attached to preserving the traditions and values of African cultures. The African charter is unique in the world because of its emphasis on "people's rights." Although the charter fails to define the concept of "people" explicitly, it seeks to preserve the traditional African social concept that the individual is not considered independent from society, but is subordinated to the group. This view, while obviously different from the individualistic Western approach and the collectivist outlook of socialist states, is grounded in the belief that the group has rights and that as a result individuals owe a duty to the group or to the state. This emphasis reflects the African belief that there can be no opposition between rights and duties, between the individual and the community.

To a Western observer the African charter is complicated by reason of its ambiguities and weaknesses. It does not provide for a court, apparently because of an African feeling that conciliation is much to be preferred to confrontation. The charter, moreover, provides for strict confidentiality, thus depriving the commission of one of the most important instruments in human rights work—the opportunity to influence public opinion.

The African charter seems to enshrine a third generation of human rights—the rights of people; these rights are apparently to be sought simultaneously with the first and second generation of rights in the economic and political order. Although the work of the Center for Human Rights in Addis Ababa cannot begin to be compared with the work done for human rights at Strasbourg and San Jose, the African initiative should not be underestimated. The efforts of Africans have stirred interest in the Moslem and Asian world. In the near future a collective enthusiasm for internationally recognized human rights all over the Third World may bring about a moral and legal revolution comparable to the revolt against colonialism that brought some one hundred countries into the family of nations during the tumultuous three decades after the establishment of the United Nations.

The European, Latin American, and African regional agencies for human rights are not now the principal governmental agencies in their areas of the world. It is not possible to make any sound predictions as to how powerful these agencies may become in the future. But they are the embodiment of the noblest aspirations of the peoples of three continents. They supplement rather than supplant the work of the United Nations. They are available to the citizens of ninety-nine nations. And although their inadequacies are apparent to everyone, their promise and their potential raise the hopes of every person who believes that the rule of law is the only way by which the world's five billion inhabitants can have peace and justice.

10. The Helsinki Accords and Soviet Jews

The United States, the USSR, and thirty-three other nations signed the Final Act of the Conference on Security and Cooperation in Europe on August 1, 1975. There was excitement and even jubilation in Russia, especially among dissidents and refuseniks. The full text of the three major "baskets" of this act, which came to be known as the Helsinki accords, was reprinted in *Pravda* and *Izvestia.* That Soviet leaders had agreed in the "third basket" of the document to abide by a broad-based array of rights was a source of joy to Soviet citizens and to human rights advocates all over the globe.

The thirty-two European nations, including the Holy See, that assembled in Helsinki to join the superpowers and Canada in signing the Helsinki accords pledged respect for "human rights and fundamental freedoms, including the freedom of thought, conscience, religion or belief, for all without distinction as to race, sex, language or religion." The participating states also recognized that respect for human rights "is an essential issue for the peace, justice, and well-being necessary to ensure the development of friendly relations and cooperation among themselves as among all states."

In a pledge reminiscent of Articles 55 and 56 of the United Nations Charter, the thirty-five nations of the Conference on Security and Cooperation in Europe (CSCE) pledged that they would "endeavor jointly and separately, including in cooperation with the United Nations, to promote universal and effective respect" for human rights. Even more strikingly the signatories agreed that they would "act in conformity with the purposes and principles of the Charter of the United Nations and with the Universal Declaration of Human Rights." They also pledged that they would "fulfill their obligations as set forth in the international documents and agreements in this field, including inter alia the

International Covenants on Human Rights, by which they may be bound." That pledge on the part of the United States was new; the United States had never before committed itself to abide by the United Nations covenants on political and economic rights. Consequently when President Ford in the presence of Secretary of State Henry Kissinger signed the Helsinki accords, it marked not only the culmination of detente but also a new and unprecedented step in America's commitment to human rights.

The deep concern for human rights in Eastern Europe that flowered in the Helsinki agreements had, of course, been a strong feeling in the West ever since the end of World War II, particularly with respect to the rights of individuals and families to emigrate. In the Helsinki accords that feeling coincided with the passionate desire of the Soviets to validate the national boundaries of the countries of Eastern Europe as they had existed since the end of World War II. The Soviets began as early as 1954 to agitate for the de jure legalization of the borders of the satellite nations they had helped to create. Polish Prime Minister Adam Rapacki revived the idea at the United Nations in 1964. Western Europe was cautious and critical of the idea of accepting the borders of East and West Germany, Poland, and the other "captive nations." The whole idea was dead until Willy Brandt began to campaign for a relaxation of tensions between East and West, initiating a series of diplomatic efforts that led to the Helsinki accords.

The West's concern for human rights in the Soviet Union has been deep and constant, especially since the end of World War II. On September 25, 1959, President Eisenhower told Nikita Khrushchev at Camp David that Jewish groups in the West had expressed deep concern over the inability of Soviet Jews either to have religious freedom or to emigrate to Israel. Khrushchev dismissed the matter, claiming that Jews in the Soviet Union were treated like everybody else. At a later time Secretary of State Christian Herter raised the same issue with Andrei Gromyko only to be told that it was an internal matter.

In 1963 Prime Minister Harold Wilson accused the Soviets of being "barbarians" for refusing to permit the reunion of families that had been separated during World War II. In 1954 German Chancellor Konrad Adenauer visited Moscow, where he refused to discuss the establishment of diplomatic relations until Soviet leaders agreed to repatriate Russians of German origin still living in labor camps. On August 29, 1954, the Soviet Presidium ordered the full rehabilitation of nearly two million German nationals.

Concerns such as these prompted the West to agree to sign the forty-thousand word Helsinki document with its long list of human rights. President Ford might well have declined to sign the long-pending Helsinki accords. Reason enough not to sign it, many American conservatives argued at the time, was the fact that the document validated forever the borders of Eastern Europe. The national bewilderment in the months immediately after the fall of Saigon might well have tempted President Ford to move away both from detente and from the Helsinki agreement, which specifically dedicates itself to the "continuation of detente."

I witnessed the hope the Helsinki accords inspired among Russians when I visited Moscow and Leningrad shortly after the accords were signed. Anatoly Scharansky, my guide and translator in Moscow, was exultant over the accords. This dynamic young Soviet computer professional took me to visit Dr. Andrei Sakharov, an eminent Soviet physicist who would soon receive the Nobel Peace Prize. In December of that same year Dr. Sakharov, in accepting the Nobel, echoed sentiments he had expressed to me in August 1975 in his Moscow apartment. Dr. Sakharov stated that in the Helsinki accords, "for the first time official expression is given to a nuanced approach which appears to be the only possible one for a solution of international security problems." "Helsinki contains," Dr. Sakharov continued, "fresh possibilities [if] the democracies maintain a unified and consistent attitude."

Although I was elated at the joy over the Helsinki accords expressed by Anatoly Scharansky, Dr. Sakharov, and several other dissidents I met in the Soviet Union, I doubt if they or anyone anticipated the explosive effect the Helsinki document would have. Although the document is not a treaty and contains no enforcement mechanism, it represents a commitment to human rights by all the nations of Europe except Albania. The document ranks as one of the most significant events in the international human rights revolution of the last forty years. A dozen years after signing of the Helsinki accords one can state with some certainty that the accords were one of the major inspirations for the Solidarity movement in Poland, for democratic initiatives in Hungary, and for a new restlessness in several of the countries dominated by the USSR.

THE CONFERENCES THAT FOLLOWED HELSINKI

One of the finest but most frustrating features of the Helsinki accords is the establishment of regular meetings between all the signatories. In 1977 the thirty-five nations convened in Belgrade, where the United States delegation was chaired by former UN Ambassador Arthur Goldberg. In sessions the like of which had never occurred before in Europe, the countries figuratively examined each others' consciences with respect to human rights. The process was shaky but salutary. In Madrid in 1980 the process was more sophisticated, although still cumbersome because decisions could be reached only by consensus.

As a congressional participant in the Madrid conference in 1980, I witnessed the remarkable process the Helsinki documents had created. The sessions were attended by twelve hundred journalists and many nongovernmental human rights groups. Twenty-seven of the thirty-five Helsinki signatories condemned the invasion of Afghanistan; only the Warsaw Pact nations voted no. The delegates noted the imprisonment in Prague of the leaders of the Charter 77 movement—a human rights group created in response to the Helsinki accords—and lamented with bitterness the jailing of all the monitors of the Helsinki accords in the Soviet Union and in the Warsaw Pact nations.

Although participants were disappointed over the lack of consensus on several issues, most agreed that the process itself was almost a miracle. Sixteen members of NATO, the seven Warsaw Pact nations, and twelve neutral or nonaligned European governments had, almost for the first time in forty years, come together to talk about human rights. Participants at Madrid also felt that the Helsinki process was now indestructible, even if the Soviets continued to stonewall. Fearing Soviet withdrawal from the process in response to criticism, some participants from the NATO nations suggested that the rhetoric against the Kremlin be muted.

The next meeting in Stockholm in 1986 centered on the reporting of military activities in Europe, a topic the Soviets especially wished to consider. The Stockholm Conference on Confidence and Security Building Measures was quite successful. Although not a single tank or gun was eliminated, the NATO and Warsaw Pact nations agreed to notify the other side of exercises and movements involving specific numbers of soldiers; both sides also agreed to send observers if the military exercises exceeded agreed-upon numbers. Western diplomats, although somewhat frustrated because the Helsinki process had been detoured from its original emphasis on human rights, were pleased that the new reporting requirements would make it more difficult, for example, for the Soviet Union to repeat the kind of intimidating military maneuvers it carried out around Poland in 1981 when Solidarity was at the height of its power.

The Stockholm talks resumed in Vienna in late 1986. Many of the delegates expressed the hope of returning to a discussion of the human rights issues contained in the "third basket" of the Final Act rather than to a discussion of European security, although it was generally conceded that the difficulties related to security were inseparable from problems connected with human rights.

The Helsinki process is at worst a forum where the superpowers can talk. If the Soviets appear to be unyielding, they at least hear the grievances of the West on topics such as freedom of the press, the right to travel without restrictions, the reunification of families, and the other rights guaranteed in the Helsinki accords.

But the Helsinki process is also a new forum for the neutral nations of Europe. For thirty-five years before the Helsinki process began in 1975, Finland, Sweden, Austria, Switzerland, Yugoslavia, Malta, Liechtenstein, Cyprus, and San Marino were largely without any voice in the tense altercations between the Warsaw Pact and NATO. The Helsinki process changed that. Switzerland has stated that for the first time it has a forum where, because of the rule of consensus adopted in Helsinki and practiced in Belgrade, Madrid, and Stockholm, it has full equality. It now has a place where it can discuss problems related to divided families and refugees and can enter into multilateral agreements on topics such as tourism.

Sweden has noted the very important role the neutral and non-aligned nations have played in negotiating disputes between the

West and the East in the Helsinki process. The Holy See has expressed its gratitude to the Helsinki process, which has been useful in connection with the rights of seminarians and priests in countries of Eastern Europe and in negotiations about disputes concerning the ownership or the operation of churches in Eastern Europe.

Cyprus, Finland, Malta, and Austria have all stressed the promise and potential of the Helsinki process; they very much want the United States to continue the Helsinki talks because, however ponderous, time-consuming, and frustrating they may be, they are one way by which these nations can be heard above the decibels of the East-West fury.

These nations are not a third bloc; they do not desire affiliation with or privileges from either side. But they now for the first time have a right to be heard and, because of the rule of consensus, a right to prevent an East-West agreement inimical to the interests of the nonaligned countries. These nations recognize that the Helsinki process is very young and that its future in Europe could, with the enthusiastic collaboration of private human rights organizations, be enormously important.

MONITORING HUMAN RIGHTS ABUSES IN EASTERN EUROPE AND THE SOVIET UNION

The Helsinki accords opened up to the West the possibility of at least monitoring conditions in Eastern Europe and reproaching the USSR when its actions run counter to commitments made at Helsinki. In the task of monitoring conditions Western human rights advocates found an ally in the Helsinki groups that sprang up in the USSR and Eastern Europe following the Helsinki accords. On May 12, 1976, Yuri Orlov, a physicist, called a press conference in Moscow to announce the formation of the Moscow Committee to Promote Observance of the Helsinki Accords, which came to be known as the Moscow Group. Dr. Orlov dreamed that in all of the thirty-five countries that signed the Helsinki accords there would eventually be groups to monitor each country's records on human rights. Monitors would be protected because the accords provided for regular review conferences at which each nation's performance would be evaluated in a public forum.

Nine months after he formed the Moscow group Yuri Orlov was in jail. Yelena Bonner, an active member of the Moscow Group and the wife of Dr. Sakharov, was eventually sent with her husband into internal exile in Gorki. Anatoly Scharansky, another charter member, was sent to jail for alleged spying; he served nine years, nearly five of them in solitary confinement. In 1986 he was allowed to go to Israel to rejoin his wife, Avital. Dr. Orlov was confined to prison or to exile until his abrupt and unexpected release in September 1986 to go to the West.

A sixty-page booklet put out in 1986 by Helsinki Watch, a private American human rights group, chronicles the fate and the current status of the twenty-two people who were members of the Moscow Group during the six years and four months of its existence. Twelve members were tried and sentenced. The others met less drastic punishment, but all were repressed, and as a result the group disbanded.

Despite what befell the Moscow group, the idea launched by Yuri Orlov caught fire in the Soviet satellite nations. Charter 77 was founded in Czechoslovakia in January 1977 and the first Polish Helsinki Watch Group, which operates underground, was formed in Poland in September 1979. In September 1982 an umbrella group—the International Helsinki Federation for Human Rights—was established; it now has ten member groups in Europe and is headquartered in Vienna.

Another promising spin-off of the Helsinki process was the establishment in 1976 by the United States Congress of the bicameral and bipartisan Commission on Security and Cooperation in Europe. This independent agency, made up of nine senators, nine members of the House of Representatives, and one official each from the Departments of State, Commerce, and Defense, has a mandate to study and encourage programs to implement the provisions of the Helsinki accords. It has done its work for a decade with devotion and dedication. It has conducted hearings, published reports, traveled to Eastern Europe, and sensitized Congress and the country to the always unfolding implications of the document the United States agreed to on August 1, 1975. Its work is advanced by the semiannual report of the State Department on the implementation of the Helsinki Final Act. These reports contain valuable information about the state of the wide range of rights agreed to by the Helsinki nations. The reports focus on the free flow of information, ideas, and people among the participating countries as well as the promotion of cultural and educational exchanges.

The massive amount of information made available by Congress and the State Department with respect to the Helsinki accords, offers unprecedented documentation of the status of human rights in Eastern Europe. Although it may be no closer to solving the human rights problems of Warsaw Pact countries, the West at least knows more acutely than ever before the extent and depth of those problems. A review of some of the developments in countries from Bulgaria to the USSR will illustrate how the struggle for human rights is affecting the life of those nations that in varying degrees are under the domination of the Kremlin.

In Bulgaria, Turks, who are Moslems, constitute 10 percent of the total population. But the rulers in Bulgaria, deeply concerned about the spread of fundamentalist Islam, have closed or destroyed thirteen hundred mosques. Turks, moreover, are required to change their names before or at the time of their marriage. The rulers of Bulgaria appear determined to destroy the cultural identity of the Turks in Bulgaria; they use the government-controlled media to bring about that objective. Clearly the authorities in Bulgaria, in their desire to form a united socialist nation, are violating several of the commitments Bulgaria made in signing the Helsinki accords.

The people of Czechoslovakia and indeed of the world will never forget the 1968 Soviet invasion designed to crush the "Prague Spring." But the desire for freedom was not crushed; it was revived by the Helsinki agreements and the flowering in 1977 of Charter 77, which had a thousand signatories. The group published a regular bulletin for several years urging compliance with the promises made in the Helsinki decrees. In 1984 the police raided the headquarters of Charter 77, destroying all books and pamphlets.

Although freedom of religion is guaranteed in the constitution of Czechoslovakia and the Helsinki accords, the eleven million

Catholics and one million Protestants in Czechoslovakia endure repression. Priests and pastors must be licensed by the government and few licenses are granted. Five hundred priests have been clandestinely ordained in the past several years. The Czech government refused permission to Pope John Paul II to visit Prague for the 1100th anniversary of the death of St. Methodius, stating that Czechoslovakia has no diplomatic relations with the Vatican. The government of Czechoslovakia has sought to control or subvert religion for its own purposes. It has helped in the formation of a pro-regime Catholic group named Pacem in Terris—a group condemned by Cardinal Tomasek.

Violations of the Helsinki principles are numerous in East Germany. Since the erection of the Berlin wall in August 1961 there has been persistent pressure to deter Germans from emigrating to West Germany. Although a total of 268,000 have emigrated since 1961, 500,000 applications to leave are pending. Political prisoners are estimated to number from 7,000 to 10,000. Academic freedom is restricted, textbooks are controlled, and the freedom to gather in public is curtailed. The 47 percent of the citizenry who are Lutheran and the 8 percent who are Catholic speak out, although some peace activists have been expelled. In 1977 the church was given greater access to radio and television, authorization was granted for some 150 Christian publications, and permission to build new churches was announced.

Hungarians have more freedom to travel abroad than citizens of any other Warsaw Pact nation. In 1977 the only rabbinical seminary in Eastern Europe, located in Hungary, celebrated its one hundredth anniversary with Jewish leaders from all over the world. In 1985 Budapest hosted the cultural forum of the Conference on Security and Cooperation in Europe—the first time any Warsaw Pact nation ever allowed such an event. Susan Sontag and other Americans participated. In 1985, Hungary allowed the Reverend Billy Graham to conduct a worship service before fifteen thousand Hungarians in Budapest—the first time Graham has been allowed in any Warsaw Pact nation. In granting the permission the government called its invitation "a projection of the Helsinki spirit to the religious field." Despite such relaxing of restrictions, the authorities in Hungary are afraid of the church, especially in view of the fact that many young people are participating in Church events because they perceive the church as a friend of freedom. The government is also afraid of the strong peace movement in Hungary.

The United States imposed sanctions on Poland after Poland's government declared martial law in December 1981. Although martial law was lifted on July 22, 1983, repression continues in Poland. In December 1983 a state of emergency was declared; this gave unprecedented power to the police and increased the jurisdiction of the military courts. Although the state has a monopoly over freedom of expression there are many active and independent publishing activities. Although it seems clear that the secret police murdered Father Jerzy Popueluszko, the Jaruzelski regime does seem somehow to respond to pleas for decency. In 1984 the government gave amnesty to 35,000 prisoners and issued 355,000 passports to persons visiting the West. It has adopted a conciliatory attitude toward the Catholic church, perhaps out of necessity. The churches are still the only places where public gatherings can legally be held.

In 1986 Poland again released a substantial number of political prisoners. Some in America feel that the United States should now lift its sanctions, while others are opposed to Polish-American normalizing relations because of Poland's refusal to restore genuinely free trade unions. But it is hard to justify the United States giving more favorable treatment in some matters to Romania and the USSR, where the human rights situation is worse than in Poland.

The twenty-one million people of Romania have suffered a bitter fate since the Soviet Union took over that nation. In 1977 the man who tried to organize a Helsinki monitoring group was expelled and his associates were imprisoned. The government is opposed to emigration, and thousands of cases involving family reunification are unresolved. Church attendance is allowed, but only fourteen denominations are recognized and these are controlled by the state. A Hungarian minority of 1.7 million persons in Transylvania feels oppressed because of what it perceives to be forced assimilation. In 1985 Helsinki Watch issued a seventy-page report urging the United States to withdraw most favored nation status from Romania. The evidence to justify the termination of that concession was powerful.

In 1985 Yugoslavia tried six intellectuals for "conspiring to overthrow socialist authority." The state trial in Belgrade was attended by observers sponsored by the American Bar Association. The penalties were much lighter than expected; four of the six defendants were released and charges were dropped.

One can interpret the hopeful signs that the state of human rights in Eastern Europe is improving as evidence that the Helsinki process is working. The process, the spirit of detente, which was inseparable from the Helsinki process, was also working, at least until the invasion of Afghanistan in December 1978. If the occupant of the White House had not changed in January 1981, would the spirit and hopes of Helsinki have made more progress? That depends on the ultimate motivations of those who hold power in the USSR.

How can one accurately and adequately describe the attitude of the Kremlin to human rights? For some Americans the answer is simple: Soviet leaders are cruelly opposed to human rights and any statement to the contrary made by them is sheer hypocrisy and propaganda. The Soviet Union is the "evil empire"; America's role is to protect the world from any further Soviet expansionism. But how does one explain the Soviets' signing the Helsinki accords? Sheer utilitarianism is the answer. They have no intention of complying.

As attractive as this oversimplified approach might be to some, it cannot make up a rational foreign policy. It is inconsistent with the commitment the United States has made in ratifying the United Nations charter, in enacting Section 502B, and in signing the Helsinki accords. The United States has international and national commitments to protect human rights that make it morally and legally impossible for the United States to make the containment of communism the only important element in America's foreign policy.

At the same time the violations of human rights by the USSR are appalling. In Afghanistan thousands of children are being sent to the Soviet Union for ten years of education, often without the knowledge of their parents. The Soviets may have some justification, but in 1985 the United Nations Human Rights Commission, in its first formal censure of the USSR, criticized the conduct of the Soviet Union in Afghanistan. The world looks with horror at the Soviet abuses in the conduct of the war in Afghanistan—mines camouflaged so that they thereby wound many, massacres of entire villages, and torture.

Yet the USSR cannot be portrayed as singularly monstrous; the United States has much to answer for in its actions in Vietnam and now, through proxies and surrogates, in El Salvador and Nicaragua. The cruelty indulged in by the Soviets must also be seen in the light of all the paranoia they have felt for many decades. They feel surrounded by enemies. They fear more invasions like the march to Moscow by the Nazis. They feel so threatened that they continue to jam the programs of the Voice of America and Radio Liberty. They accredit thirty-one journalists in Moscow but bar the *Wall Street Journal.* The nation's imperialist bureaucracy is controlled by a small clique. Despite all these grievances the United States and thirty-three other nations agreed to sign the Helsinki accords because they recognized that the Kremlin, for all its paranoia and barbarism, can sometimes be persuaded or pressured to comply with some internationally recognized human rights. And that is what the Kremlin did when in 1970 it began to allow Soviet Jews to emigrate.

THE EXODUS OF SOVIET JEWS

The emigration of some 260,000 Soviet Jews in the past two decades has to be classified as the most extraordinary and even awesome victory for human rights since the United Nations charter and the UN covenants elevated the observance of human rights to a duty commanded by international law. The more than two million Jews who reside in the Soviet Union have felt almost imprisoned since the gates of escape were closed at the time of the revolution in 1917. Soviet Jews felt especially aggrieved after the establishment of Israel in 1948 made it possible for Jews from all parts of the earth to make *aliyah* to Israel.

In 1963 I visited Israel for the first time. At the tomb of Theodor Herzl, the founder of modern Zionism, my guide almost casually said that one of the fundamental purposes of the founding of Israel was to serve as a homeland for the two or three million Soviet Jews when and if they could escape. This hoped-for migration to Israel has been called the "last Exodus." The liberation of the Jews of the Soviet Union has always been a particularly high priority for many of the founders of Israel who had roots in Russia, Poland, and other East European nations. They worked in every possible way to bring about the "last Exodus."

In the West surprisingly little was known about Soviet Jews until Elie Wiesel, after a visit to the Soviet Union, published *The Jews of Silence* in 1967. This book drew world attention to the plight of Soviet Jews, who comprise some 20 percent of all the Jews in the world. The Jews of the Soviet Union escaped the Holocaust, but their condition was deplorable. They had experienced the decimation of Jewish culture, the closing of synagogues, a ban on the study of the Hebrew language, and the humiliation of being required to carry an identity card stating that they were Jewish. I witnessed firsthand the heartrending condition of Jews in the Soviet Union when I visited them in Leningrad, Moscow, and other cities in 1975 (after the Soviets had twice denied me, a United States congressman, a visa). The deep faith in Judaism that so many had was nothing less than a miracle of grace. I saw more profoundly than ever before the mysterious ways in which the God of Abraham, Isaac, and Jacob speaks to those born in that biblical tradition. The Soviet Jews whom I met in Russia in 1975 and the Jews from Russia whom I met in Israel in the 1970s and 1980s could not explain in words why they had a desire and determination to go to Israel. These Jews all recognized a call from God, a reawakening of faith, a mysterious and mystical compulsion.

In 1971 the First World Conference on Soviet Jewry in Brussels launched a vigorous campaign to pressure the USSR into releasing Soviet Jews who wished to emigrate. The Soviets complained bitterly to the Belgium government about the convening of the conference on the conditions of Jews in Russia. Furious editorials in *Izvestia* and *Pravda* denounced the conference, while a delegation of Soviet Jews, beholden to the Kremlin, held public meetings in Brussels to declare that the conference was not necessary.

Brussels I, attended by nine hundred Jews from all over the world, had its impact. The emigration of Jews in the early 1970s was significant, even spectacular, considering that the right to leave had never previously been granted. In the five years between Brussels I in 1971 and Brussels II in 1976, 115,000 Soviet

Jews received visas to leave. But the total of 33,000 allowed to leave in 1973 decreased to about 12,000 in 1976.

The second Brussels conference was conducted after the Soviet authorities had signed the Helsinki accords. Hope was high even though on February 19, 1976, *Pravda* defended the Kremlin's record on human rights against the French Communists' charges of repression in the USSR. The Soviets reiterated the standard contention that 98.4 percent of all those who asked to leave in the 1970–75 period were permitted to do so.

Along with some forty Christians I joined approximately thirteen hundred Jews from an amazing array of nations at Brussels II. I had been encouraged and inspired by a long talk with Dr. Sakharov in Moscow in August 1975. One of the many things he told me was of his strong conviction that "only the Christians of America can liberate the Jews of Russia." Dr. Sakharov saw what Brussels I had accomplished in influencing world opinion and seemed to feel that it might have helped to induce Soviet authorities to sign the Helsinki pact.

Towards the end of the Brussels II conference the Christians present expressed their desire to make a statement paralleling and supporting the conclusions of the Jewish delegates. It was accepted with great emotion by Golda Meir, who said that on the issue of Soviet Jews "we have always been alone." The Christians' statement promised that "this generation of Christians will not be silent . . . in the struggle to prevent the cultural and spiritual annihilation of the Jews in the Soviet Union." Delicately noting that Christians too suffered in the Soviet Union, the Christians declared:

We Christians . . . keenly aware of the plight of all persons of conscience in the USSR and especially pained by the harassment and persecution of our Christian brothers and sisters, nonetheless are convinced that the oppressed condition of our Jewish brothers and sisters is unique and in all specifics more rigorous than that faced by the Christian communities.

Golda Meir, in accepting this statement, asserted the determination of Jews within and outside the Soviet Union.

We cannot accept that teaching Hebrew is counter- revolutionary. We cannot accept that 3 million Jews have no right to have a theatre, have no newspaper. The second greatest power in the world—what are you gain-ing from this policy. . . . We just refuse to disappear. No matter how strong and brutal and ruthless the forces against us may be—here we are. Millions of bodies broken, buried alive, burned to death. But never has anyone been able to succeed in breaking the spirit of our people.

Brussels II lamented the outrages inflicted on the refuseniks of the Soviet Union. It complained of their expulsion from institutes of learning, their loss of pensions, and the lack of any orderly and predictable procedure for migration. But the atmosphere of Brussels II was upbeat and hopeful. One of the themes at Brussels II was a powerful quotation from Thomas Jefferson that summed up the essence of what was at stake: "Our ancestors possessed a right which nature has given to all men, of departing from the country which chance—not choice—has placed them."

The number of Soviet Jews allowed to leave Russia plummeted from 51,320 in 1979 to 9,447 in 1981 and to 2,680 in 1982. This may have been due to the deterioration of detente after the invasion of Afghanistan or to a slackening of effort on the part of Jews and their allies in the international human rights movement. Or the Kremlin may just have determined that it would no longer allow some of its best and brightest to leave Russia, especially when a large percentage of them were going to the United States and not to Israel.

An atmosphere of gloom and doom pervaded the Third World Conference on Soviet Jewry held in March 1985 in Jerusalem. During the conference Jews who had recently arrived from Russia importuned me to help them to bring out their spouses, their parents, and their children. These emigres were angry and confused that emigration from the Soviet Union had virtually ceased in 1984. They distrusted the Soviets too much to urge a return to detente. They wanted to blame the Reagan administration for the sharp reversal in the future of Soviet Jews, but deep down they approved of the Reagan administration's belligerence toward the Soviet Union. That government had repressed them and now was detaining their loved ones, contrary to every instinct of humanity and the commitments the Soviet Union had solemnly made at Helsinki.

Many other conferees shared the desperation of the recent emigres. Speaker after speaker reminded the distinguished world audience that continued and persistent advocacy of their cause was the only successful way to proceed—as it had been in the previous fifteen years. But others were less sanguine; they were trying to prepare themselves for the possibility that there would be little, if any, additional emigration and that the dream of the "last Exodus" was over for at least another generation. One of the most consoling features for both Jews and Christians at the conference was the support from Christians for the continued emigration of Soviet Jews. Although there was bafflement and division over the many reasons for the virtual halt to the emigration of Soviet Jews, all at the conference in Jerusalem recognized that public advocacy must be continued and, indeed, accelerated.

The epic of the emigration of more than a quarter of a million Soviet Jews dramatizes what a worldwide movement can do. It would of course be better if Jews and everyone in the Soviet Union could have freedom to practice their religion and develop their cultural heritage within their own country, as provided for in the Helsinki accords. But in the absence of a guarantee that religion and cultural identities will be respected in the Soviet Union, Jews and others have a right to emigrate that is protected by international law. The Jewish situation is unique because Jews have a claim to join the ingathering of exiles Israel represents and made possible. The departure of Jews is, of course, an embarrassment to Soviet officials when confronted by other ethnic groups who also desire either to be able to assert their cultural identity within Russia or to go elsewhere where they can do so. Could it be that the bureaucrats in the Kremlin have concluded that if they continue to allow Jews to depart, the protests from the many other ethnic groups will become uncontrollable?

That is one of the many mysteries surrounding Soviet intentions on human rights. But at least the signing of the Helsinki accords by the Kremlin and the granting of permission to emigrate to 260,000 Jews in the years from 1970 to the present indicate some flexibility on the part of Soviet leaders.

The Helsinki process will continue. Its meetings in Vienna in 1986 and 1987 gave some promise that all the talk and the search for consensus are not unavailing. The September 1986 release from prison of Yuri Orlov, the founder of the Helsinki monitors in Moscow, might be a sign that some Soviet authorities feel pressured to fulfill the promises they made at Helsinki. The unique

Congressional Commission on Security in Europe and the biannual reports of the State Department continue to document the degree of compliance with the Helsinki accords. Helsinki Watch, along with Freedom House, both aggressive nongovernmental agencies devoted to human rights, will also help to focus attention on the promises of Helsinki.

The preamble of the Helsinki accords expresses the desire of the participating nations to bring about "the spiritual enrichment of the human personality [and a] broader dissemination of knowledge irrespective of their politics, economic and social systems." Human rights transcend political ideology, the preamble affirms; human rights rise above the question of whether nations are capitalist or socialist in their economies. The preamble to the Helsinki accords is a daring statement. It seeks a way to reconcile East and West, capitalism and socialism. Like the United Nations charter, this sentiment is based on the faith that respect for human rights can unite nations and people who are otherwise deeply divided by economic and cultural differences.

11. South Africa, Pariah Nation

Those who have watched with enthusiasm and even exaltation the international gains made for human rights have their hopes confounded when they confront South Africa. Almost every moral and legal remedy available to the world community to induce or to compel the observance of human rights has been employed against South Africa in the past forty years. But some twenty-six million blacks are still segregated and repressed by the ruling class of some four million whites. The General Assembly and the Security Council of the United Nations, the World Court at The Hague, and virtually every international and religious group in the world has condemned apartheid. But it continues to exist, defiant of international law, the opinion of civilized humankind, and economic boycotts that continue to get tougher on Pretoria. It is an abomination, a form of slavery, another version of the superior race theory embraced by Nazism, and an offense particularly to the fifty-one nations of black Africa.

When I first visited Soweto in 1978 and talked to black and white leaders in South Africa I had the hope that somehow the demise of apartheid could be worked out. The gradual transition that formed the nation of Zimbabwe from the colony of Rhodesia gave hope to the world that somehow a pluralistic society could be born in the beautiful and resource-rich land of South Africa.

But time has not substantiated that hope. Indians and coloreds have been given at least a symbolic role in South Africa in the tricameral parliament, but not blacks. When I visited South Africa in 1978 I spent a good deal of time with a black priest who had been "banned" by the government. Father Smangalsio Mkhatshwa, a most engaging diocesan priest with a doctorate in theology from Louvain, was forbidden to speak in public because he had allegedly been organizing young people against the government. I wrote articles about Father Mkhatshwa and sent them to him. Some five years later I met with Father Mkhatshwa in Washington. The ban against him had been lifted partly because of my articles and also because of the pressure I brought on the then-ambassador from South Africa to the United States. After traveling and speaking in the United States Father Mkhatshwa returned to his position as the executive secretary of the Southern African Conference of Catholic Bishops. Contrary to our hopes he was again banned and jailed. In 1986 he was brutally tortured and held without charges.

In November 1986 the officers of the Southern African Conference of Catholic Bishops had a meeting with the South African president, P. W. Botha, and members of his administration. The bishops requested the meeting to discuss the crisis in the country. The president of the conference, Archbishop Denis Hurley of Durban, reported at a press conference in Pretoria that the two-hour meeting had been "frustrating and unsatisfactory." According to Archbishop Hurley, President Botha spoke about the government's concern with the Communist threat and with the African National Congress (ANC), which, Botha claimed, was controlled by the "Communist Party in England."

One of the principal items on the bishops' agenda was the detention without trial of thousands of South Africans, including many clergy; one of those detained was Father Mkhatshwa, who had been in prison since June 12, 1986. President Botha responded that interference from church personnel would not be tolerated, and his warning to church leaders was reported on the government- controlled broadcasting corporation the evening of the meeting. The dealings the government has had with the Catholics of South Africa illustrate the brutal and adamant determination of the government to stop every religious, moral, or political movement that would undermine apartheid.

The continued affront to human rights in South Africa is undoubtedly a top priority for human rights activists in the entire world. It is a source of profound embarrassment and sorrow to everyone associated with human rights that the entire legal, political, and moral machinery of the world has not in forty years been able to alter the approach of the one nation that on principle insists that black people be separated from whites. The segregation insisted upon by the government in Pretoria has been on the agenda of the UN General Assembly in virtually every one of its sessions over the past forty years. Apartheid has been condemned and excoriated in every available forum for many years. Virtually all nations, including the United States, have observed the arms boycott against South Africa imposed by the United Nations in the early 1960s.

South Africa's new constitution, adopted in 1984, was characterized by the United Nations as a further entrenchment of apartheid. The new constitution was rejected by both the General Assembly in 1983 and by the Security Council in August 1984, which declared the new constitution to be null and void. The UN General Assembly has also condemned the policy of the forced removals of black people. In 1984 it recognized the national liberation movement in South Africa as the "authentic representatives" of the people; it urged all governments to "take appropriate action . . . to assist the oppressed people of South Africa in their legitimate struggle for national liberation."

Every informed person in the West has been troubled for many, many years about South Africa. One grew up with Alan Paton's 1948 novel *Cry the Beloved Country*, in which a sensitive and religious person graphically portrayed the rise of Afrikaner nationalism and apartheid.

UNITED STATES SANCTIONS AGAINST SOUTH AFRICA

The murder of Steve Biko in the 1970s prompted the establishment of a congressional caucus on South Africa. The grim events in South Africa from Sharpeville to Soweto, the emergence of Zimbabwe, and the fight against apartheid by Ambassador Andrew Young and the Carter administration all deepened the anger and antagonism Americans felt toward South Africa. But few could have foreseen that the hatred for apartheid was strong enough to prompt the series of events that culminated in Congress overriding President Reagan's veto of a bill imposing severe sanctions against South Africa. The sustained anti-apartheid pressure in the United States—along with thousands of other anti-apartheid activities throughout the world—persuaded Congress to override President Reagan's veto of a bill prescribing economic sanctions against South Africa. The override was uniquely overwhelming; the vote on October 2, 1986, was 313 to

83 in the House and 78 to 21 in the Senate. No such rejection of a president on a fundamental matter of foreign policy had occurred since Congress in 1973 overrode President Nixon's veto of the War Powers Resolution.

The deep convictions that prompted the override represent a high point in the anti-apartheid struggle. But it remains to be seen whether economic sanctions by the United States will change the course of history in South Africa.

The story of the campaign for economic sanctions confirms that the demand for the observance of internationally recognized human rights breaks out in unlikely places and for unpredicted reasons. The idea of the preciousness and sacredness of human rights is like the seed described in the gospel. It falls on barren soil as well as on fertile soil. Where it will produce fruit is unpredictable. But it will bear fruit.

Pressure on Congress began when on Thanksgiving of 1984 a dynamic Washington group, TransAfrica, under the leadership of Randall Robinson, began to picket the South African embassy in Washington. The arrests of black demonstrators caught the attention of the press and for a whole year black and white demonstrators each day committed a technical trespass and were arrested and jailed. In 1985 I participated in these demonstrations. I came closer to the South African embassy than local law allows and was, almost by prearrangement, arrested, booked, and confined for a few hours. It was my first experience in anything involving civil disobedience. I am not certain that I was thoroughly persuaded of its usefulness, but the oppressive situation in South Africa and the judgment of those seeking to prompt the United States to do something about it induced me to join the hundreds of lawyers, public officials, and educators who peacefully picketed the embassy of South Africa each day for twelve months.

I feel certain that the people who demonstrated for freedom in South Africa remember, as I do, every single moment of the hours of detention. I am certain also that the demonstrators wonder whether their activities helped to bring about the passage by Congress of rather tough economic sanctions against South Africa. Undoubtedly the demonstrations helped. But they were but one more factor added to the years of protests against apartheid.

On January 14, 1985, South Africa's ambassador in Washington called together a group of some thirty persons, including myself, with whom he wanted to discuss the emerging confrontation between his embassy and human rights activists. Ambassador Bernardus G. Fourie was clearly frightened. He had been South Africa's ambassador to the United Nations. He had argued and fought for apartheid for over thirty years but clearly had never been as frustrated or upset as he was in January 1985. Everyday he read in the *Washington Post* of the prestigious people who were daily being arrested outside his embassy. The ambassador tried to minimize the impact of the demonstrations of the last two months. He put forward what he conceived to be good things happening in his country; the educational budget, he reported, had for the first time exceeded the military budget. But he was challenged by speaker after speaker. He proffered limp answers to questions about the homelands, the denial of citizenship to blacks, the enforcement of the pass laws, and the refusal of South Africa to leave Namibia.

My notes on that dinner meeting kept raising questions: Can he sincerely believe what he is telling us? Is he just terrified that all these things are happening on his watch? Does he think that anyone will believe him when he claims that the Southern African government is changing as rapidly as it can? I told the ambassador privately that I and countless American Catholics were following closely the forthcoming trial of Archbishop Denis Hurley for alleged violations of the law forbidding the teaching of racial equality. I was pleased to see that the trial of Archbishop Hurley was subsequently called off. Once again, whether this specific plea made any difference is open to question.

Ambassador Fourie tried almost desperately to turn back the rising tide in favor of economic sanctions. South Africa certainly did all it could to make the case against economic sanctions. Pretoria hired lobbyists to argue against the mounting feeling that if the United States cut off trade with Poland or Nicaragua for ideological reasons, it should also terminate all trade with South Africa.

In February 1985 I was happy to participate in efforts that prompted the 425 members of the House of Delegates of the American Bar Association to pass a resolution opposing apart-

heid and urging the United States government to take appropriate action to oppose apartheid. The subsequent testimony by an
American Bar Association spokesperson before the United States
Senate on behalf of economic sanctions against South Africa was
reportedly a very significant factor in the Senate's approval of
sanctions.

Anti-apartheid pressure mounted in 1985. Students protested
investment of college endowments in corporations with operations in South Africa, and many colleges divested their funds.
Bishop Desmond Tutu became a household word. The states of
New Jersey and California divested all stocks in corporations that
traded with South Africa. The United States Catholic Conference, representing three hundred Catholic bishops, withdrew all
of its funds from entities that did business with South Africa.
Conflicts in South Africa that hitherto had been almost over-
looked were featured regularly, almost nightly, on television
news. The American Bar Association invited two dozen South African jurists to a series of seminars and events that attracted wide
attention.

The drumbeat against South Africa continued into 1986. To
the astonishment of everyone the Anti-Apartheid Act sponsored
by Democratic Congressman Ronald Dellums of California
passed the House unanimously on a voice vote. The measure, the
strongest of any major sanctions bill ever proposed against South
Africa, prohibited any United States individual or corporation
from investing in, importing from, or exporting to South Africa.
It required the immediate withdrawal or divestment of all United
States government assets currently in South Africa. It banned the
imports of all articles from or produced in South Africa. All land-
ing rights were denied to any aircraft owned by the South African
government. The penalties were stiff—up to $1 million for cor-
porations, up to $50,000 or five years imprisonment or both for
individuals. The bill passed by the House would have required the
280 American companies that employ 66,000 people in South Africa to cease operations and forego transactions worth $1.8 bil-
lion annually.

Opponents of economic sanctions argued that sanctions do not
work, that they hurt the very people they are intended to help,
and that they would strengthen the extremist elements in South

African society. But the arguments against sanctions persuaded fewer and fewer in Congress and the country. Despite all the pressure of the Reagan administration, seeking to justify and continue its policy of constructive engagement, political opinion continued to shift in favor of severe penalties against South Africa. On June 17, 1986, the very day the House passed a surprisingly sweeping bill mandating economic sanctions, the United States, joined by Great Britain, vetoed a UN Security Council resolution that would have imposed limited economic sanctions against South Africa.

The bill passed by the Senate was not as strong as the sweeping measure that cleared the House. But the Senate bill, which with a few minor alterations became law, was stronger than many would have preferred. The ban on trade with South Africa forbids all new United States investments and bank loans, but companies will still be allowed to reinvest their profits. Imports from South Africa of iron, farm products, and other items are prohibited. South African airlines, which carried 95,000 passengers to the United States in 1985, may no longer land.

Several factors brought about the enactment of these bills in both chambers and the override of the presidential veto. Civil rights groups in the United States had made the vote into a litmus test of a person's fidelity to the objectives of the civil rights movement in America. The churches exercised pressure. But above all it was the long-developing pressure of the human rights movement that made it almost impossible for members of Congress to cast a negative vote on a measure that, despite its emphasis on economic sanctions, was meant as an expression of moral opposition to apartheid.

The pullout of United States corporations from South Africa began shortly after the astonishing override of the president's veto. General Electric, General Motors, IBM, and other highly visible corporations walked away from South Africa. They had fought for years to comply with the fair employment principles authored by the Reverend Leon Sullivan but ultimately came to the conclusion that, for a variety of pragmatic and political reasons, they should leave South African trade routes to others. The Interfaith Center on Corporate Responsibility, an umbrella group of more than two hundred Roman Catholic and Protestant groups, hailed the departure of the giant corporations because it sent a message to other American corporations that "it is bad business to do business with South Africa."

The anti-apartheid legislation enacted by Congress in late 1986 might be limited by the loopholes it contains. But it gave a signal to corporations everywhere that they might be well advised to avoid the declining profits and escalating troubles in South Africa. Unfortunately the bill did little to curb the enormous profits that South Africa makes on its exports of gold. One proposal outlined in the conservative *London Economist* suggested that if the richest nations of the world, including the United States, put up for sale their immense reserves of gold, the world price of gold would tumble—with dire financial consequences to the economy of South Africa. Apparently no one expects rich nations to put all their gold on the market.

SOUTH AFRICAN RECALCITRANCE

It is ironic that the worst affront to human rights in the world, the government of South Africa, came into being in its present form in 1948, the very year the United Nations initiated its seminal document, the Universal Declaration of Human Rights. The contents of that document in all its emanations have been applied to South Africa in every available form. Even though efforts to apply the principles of that document in South Africa have not been satisfactory, one can take some consolation in thinking that if it were not for the human rights machinery of the United Nations, the situation in South Africa would conceivably be worse than it is now.

In October 1985 representatives of the forty-nine British Commonwealth nations came together to try to resolve what to do about South Africa. An Eminent Persons Group (EPG) was chosen to try to initiate a dialogue within South Africa and to "leave nothing undone that might contribute to peaceful change" in South Africa. Over the course of six months the group conducted more than twenty meetings with all the significant leaders in South Africa, including Nelson Mandela and other leaders of the African National Congress, the Pan-African Congress, and the Frontline states. The group developed a plan for a dialogue between the South African government and the black majority, which it presented to the government of South Africa in March 1986.

In June 1986 the Eminent Persons Group made public its conclusion that the South African government is "not yet prepared to negotiate fundamental change, nor to countenance the creation of genuine democratic structures, nor to face the prospect of the end of white domination and white power in the foreseeable future." The findings of the Commonwealth group, chaired by Malcolm Fraser, prime minister of Australia from 1975 to 1983, were published in 1986 under the title "Mission to South Africa." The report, made public in London, is gloomy and almost without hope. It relates that the Botha government refused even to negotiate removing the military from the townships, releasing Nelson Mandela, lifting the ban on the ANC and the Pan-African Congress, or permitting normal political activity. Nor would the Botha government allow Nelson Mandela to communicate with other black leaders such as the chief of the Zulus, Mangosuthu Buthelezi. The government was not even willing to respond to Chief Buthelezi's opinion that Mandela's release is necessary to bring about some kind of a solution.

In the fall 1986 issue of *Foreign Affairs* Malcolm Fraser and his co-chairman, Gen. Alusegun Obasarjo of Nigeria, outlined the adamant refusal of the Botha government to consider any significant change. Pretoria insisted that the present tricameral constitution was the only vehicle for future reform and that the homelands policy was non-negotiable. In his commentary Mr. Fraser, reflecting the views of the EPG report, strongly endorsed economic sanctions against South Africa. Even if they did not work they would give a signal to the oppressed millions that they had friends throughout the world and that they should continue to hope and work for their freedom. Fraser felt that Japan and Europe would follow the lead of the United States and that commercial isolation *might* move South Africa. He stated categorically that "it is our firm view that the South African government will never be moved" by "gentle diplomacy and quiet persuasion." Fraser warned that time is running out and that "once a guerrilla struggle has commenced, it will be almost impossible to return to the negotiating table until one side becomes exhausted by long years of conflict." He concluded by pleading with America and Britain to alter their present course of inaction; if they do not, their silence will "severely limit their influence in many parts of the world."

The report of the Eminent Persons Group has not yet persuaded the English government to impose severe sanctions. The world will wait at least through 1987 to see if economic sanctions imposed by the United States will have a measurable effect on the situation in South Africa. In the meantime the moral indignation of the world against South Africa continues to deepen. Every month shocking numbers of murders are committed by the government of South Africa. The clergy in South Africa, emboldened by the Nobel Peace Prize awarded to Archbishop Tutu and by the sheer heroism of the Catholic bishops and so many others, continue to work for change in a society where the white minority owns the vast bulk of the land.

There is evidence that whites in South Africa are awakening to the urgency of their situation. In late 1986 South Africa's major white Dutch Reform Church approved a statement calling apartheid unjust. The forced separation of people cannot be seen as a prescription from the *Bible.* Such an attempt to justify it . . . must be recognized as an error and rejected." For decades the 1.4-million-member Dutch Reform Church, which represents 40 percent of all whites and 65 percent of all Afrikaners, has provided a theological justification for apartheid. Because of the church's special relationship with the ruling national party, the statement adopted on October 22, 1986, in Capetown represents a significant change.

THE FUTURE OF SOUTH AFRICA

South Africa's future is uncertain. Will there be a long-drawn-out, violent uprising? Can there be a relatively peaceful emergence of a democracy along the lines of Zimbabwe? Or is the military strength of the white minority sufficient to keep it in power for the foreseeable future?

If the code of human rights that is a part of customary international law were possessed of adequate force and sufficient sanctions, its acceptance by Pretoria could be secured. How then could international human rights be strengthened so that the rule of law could be guaranteed in South Africa? If all major nations enacted sanctions, as the United States has done, the isolation of South Africa from world commerce might force it to capitulate and grant some of the basic political and economic rights to 87 percent of its population. In the absence of alternative solutions the United States clearly has a duty to persuade other countries to join it in pressuring the Botha regime to change. But if the United States concludes that the present regime in Pretoria will not change its position on apartheid, what should the United States, in cooperation with its allies, do? That is the hardest of all the questions.

Malcolm Fraser, echoing the feelings of the Eminent Persons Group, has stated that a "much greater descent into violence is inevitable" in South Africa. He thinks that the kind of government that would emerge from a civil war of some eight to ten years' duration "would be totally radical, owing its allegiance to those countries from which it would obtain arms and support."

Although South Africa is a uniquely polarized and dangerous place, the prediction of Mr. Fraser may to some extent also be true of other nations that are struggling to throw off an authoritarian rule or have already done so. After their liberation they look to the countries that have helped them in their hour of need. Following this logic, the United States should be seeking to make friends with the black insurgents in South Africa who inevitably will one day govern South Africa. If these people perceive the United States to be allied with a government that repressed and persecuted them, they will ally themselves with nations hostile to Washington. But if, after their liberation, they can look to the White House as a proven friend, they will be anxious to move into America's orbit in the world.

The resolution of South Africa's troubles could be as relatively peaceful as the liberation of the Philippines from Marcos and Duvalier's departure from Haiti. But the resolution could also entail a struggle as bitter as the one going on in Northern Ireland or as tragic as the revolution in Iran. Of the all-white regimes that have held power in Africa, all but South Africa have yielded to some form of rule not based exclusively on the separation of people according to race. No nation so conceived can endure in the modern world where separation predicated on race is universally held to be illegal and immoral.

Paradoxically the white government in Pretoria is in many ways a prisoner of those who work for justice, of world personalities such as Archbishop Tutu, Nelson Mandela, and Mr. Buthelezi, chief of the six million Zulus. The Botha government is even frightened by a gentle and meek priest, Father Mkhatshwa. When a government's moral claim to rule is so tenuous, it must of necessity fear all challenges, great and small.

The blacks of South Africa are Christian in very profound ways. But their anger at their condition can turn into what they would describe as an anger inspired by God. They can continue to work and pray for their liberation from a form of slavery. But they can also come to the conclusion that their liberation can only be won through violence. Archbishop Tutu, who has always advocated nonviolence, appears to be somewhat fatalistic. He is careful never to preach anything approaching hatred; he is always eloquent on the necessity of love. Yet he spoke perceptively and prophetically when he reflected that South Africa's rulers may force a violent confrontation. "I think the white ruling class is quite ready to do a Samson on us. That is, they will pull down the pillars, even if it means they perish in the process. They are really scared that we are going to treat them as they treated us."

12. Nongovernmental Human Rights Organizations

Even if an international mechanism capable of enforcing human rights standards were created, there would still be a need for private nongovernmental agencies devoted to the observance of human rights. These groups arguably would be more vigorous in the absence of a publicly financed unit officially assigned to enforce human rights standards. On the other hand, it is undeniably true that private agencies will probably never have the prestige and power they need if their views are not supported by the law and by public agencies.

The growth, almost the proliferation, of private human rights groups is one of the most amazing phenomenons in the global village since World War II. All types of national humanitarian organizations were established before the United Nations. But virtually none except the Red Cross had the dream of serving humanity across national lines. Amnesty International, established in 1961 in London, is the model and archetype of most human rights groups.

AMNESTY INTERNATIONAL

In the fall of 1960 a Catholic British lawyer, Peter Benenson, read that two students in Lisbon had been sent to jail for seven years for a small act of defiance against Portuguese dictator Antonio Salazar. Mr. Benenson decided to ask the public to bombard Portuguese authorities with letters of protest. From this effort Amnesty International was born. Mr. Benenson deliberately chose Trinity Sunday to launch it. He also noted the appropriateness of establishing Amnesty International in 1961, one hundred years after the emancipation of the slaves in America and the liberation of the serfs in Russia.

Amnesty International sends observers on missions to those

countries where human rights are being consistently violated. A trip I took for Amnesty International in November 1976 to Argentina was the beginning of many worldwide protests against the disappearances and deaths of thousands of persons in that country. Amnesty International also organizes lawyers to work for imprisoned colleagues and to present educational programs on human rights.

Amnesty International was modest in its size and aspirations before it received the 1977 Nobel Peace Prize. Since that time it has flowered into a worldwide organization with six hundred thousand members in chapters in almost every nation of the world. Its scope is restricted to political offenses against human rights. It does not enter the area of economic rights. It concentrates on the elimination of the death penalty and abolition of torture—both, it is hoped before the year 2000. The *Annual Amnesty International Report,* a catalogue of human rights violations in some 150 nations, is admired for its accuracy, its comprehensiveness, its objectivity, and its nonpolitical nature. Amnesty's files in its London headquarters, kept by a staff of over two hundred persons from some thirty countries, are global and comprehensive; because of the confidential nature of the information tight security at Amnesty International is required.

Since its founding Amnesty has worked on behalf of more than twenty-five thousand prisoners of conscience around the world. Such prisoners are detained on account of their beliefs, color, sex, ethnic origin, language, or religion. Amnesty International groups "adopt" specific prisoners, which means their members send countless letters and telegrams to the authorities detaining the prisoner of conscience. No person is adopted if he or she has used or advocated violence.

Amnesty International is scrupulous about its abhorrence of violence. When Nelson Mandela changed from nonviolent to violent opposition to the apartheid regime, Amnesty International dropped Mandela from its list of prisoners of conscience. It did, however, vow to protest if his prison conditions were deemed harsh or if he were subjected to torture.

The effectiveness of letters sent by Amnesty International members is dramatized by this statement from a released prisoner of conscience from the Dominican Republic:

When the first 200 letters came the guards gave me back my clothes. Then the next 200 letters came, and the prison director came to see me. When the next pile of letters arrived, the director got in touch with his superior. The letters kept coming and coming: 3000 of them. The president was informed. The letters kept arriving, and the president called the prison and told them to let me go.

In another case, a released prisoner of conscience from Vietnam asserted that "we could always tell when international protests were taking place...the food rations increased and the beatings were fewer. Letters from abroad were translated and passed from cell to cell, but when the letters stopped the dirty food and repression started again."

In its first twenty-five years Amnesty handled 30,000 prisoner adoption cases; 25,559 of those are now closed. the organization is hesitant and cautious about claiming any victories, but by universal consensus it is enormously beneficial for a political prisoner to be adopted by Amnesty International.

Amnesty's worldwide campaign to celebrate its twenty-fifth anniversary featured a program called "Conspiracy of Hope," a celebration held in Washington, D.C. The organization issued one of its most compelling protests against the current epidemic of torture and human rights abuses:

When you do something to help a prisoner of conscience or to try to save someone from torture, you are doing something of incalculable value— even if it may seem very modest to you. You are taking a stand for human dignity. You are saying that you refuse to accept the torture, the humiliation and the silencing of another human being. In the face of cruelty and the arrogant abuse of limitless power, you are proving—by personal example—to both the victims and their tormentors that compassion, justice and human love are still alive.

THE INTERNATIONAL COMMISSION OF JURISTS

The International Commission of Jurists founded in 1952 has asserted and vindicated the independence of judges and lawyers, an essential prerequisite for protecting human rights of citizens. American lawyers may take for granted the independence of the bench and the bar in the United States, but in dozens of nations the judiciary is either not formally independent from the other branches of government or its independence has been destroyed, often by violent tactics. the International Commission of Jurists—especially through its Geneva-based agency, the Center for the Independent Judges and Lawyers—publicizes the intimidation of judges and lawyers wherever it occurs—from South Korea to South Africa. In Argentina twenty-three lawyers were assassinated from 1974 to 1979 and over one hundred attorneys were among the "disappeared." Since 1980 scores of lawyers have been assassinated and "disappeared" in Guatemala. In Pakistan in the early 1980s lawyers opposing martial law on behalf of their clients were detained without charge.

Lawyers can also be sidelined by disbarment or suspension from practice. This has happened in Czechoslovakia, South Korea, Poland, and elsewhere. In South Africa lawyers can be "banned"—a practice that severely limits one's freedom of movement and association. If the entire legal profession is a threat to a dictator he can dissolve the bar association as President Al-Assâd of Syria did in March 1980 to punish the Syrian Bar Association (founded in 1912) for participating in a one-day protest over a prolonged "state of emergency." The mildest form of interference with attorney independence is harassment. The forms of harassment are legion. In Thailand some defense lawyers receive "funeral flowers" as hints of what a continuation of their efforts might bring about.

Judges can also be taken out of operation. In 1976, after the military seizure of Argentina, all members of the judiciary were stripped of their tenure. Approximately 80 percent were replaced. A similar mass removal occurred in Pakistan in 1977. Judges in other countries have been forced to swear pledges of loyalty to particular regimes or resign. The oaths include affirmations not to question any decision or law of the "new order." As a result all judicial review of the orders of the new government are precluded or nullified. In 1981 nine of Pakistan's highest judges, including the chief justice, were dismissed when they refused to swear allegiance to General Zia and to cease reviewing judgments of his military tribunals.

In Paraguay judges who do not follow the instructions given to them by the authorities are transferred to less important posts or removed. Possibly the simplest way to undercut the independence of the judiciary is to limit or change the jurisdiction of the courts; in South Africa this technique was followed when the government prohibited judicial inquiries into the legality of incommunicado detention.

In 1983 the International Commission of Jurists issued a five-hundred page document focusing on the use in fifteen countries of so-called "states of emergency" or "states of siege." The study focuses on the many occasions in the 1960s and 1970s when the fifteen countries being surveyed relied on a prolonged or indefinite state of emergency to suspend what remained of basic human rights and the procedures for their enforcement. Legal and political experts agree that in certain rare times of national emergency a state has the right to deviate from its human rights treaty obligations. But unless such situations are carefully and continuously monitored, there will be a vast erosion of judicial and attorney independence.

The International Commission of Jurists continues to be the leading organization in monitoring government compliance with existing international legal standards concerning the independence of the judicial process. Its work is supplemented and extended by the Network of Concerned Correspondents, a group approved by the American Bar Association in 1980. Modeled on similar programs established by the National Academy of Sciences, the Network of Concerned Correspondents assists in the preparation of political asylum applications on behalf of lawyers and judges seeking asylum outside of their country of origin. The Network collaborates closely with the International Trial Observers Project sponsored by the American Bar Association. This ABA project sends trial observers abroad in the hope that their presence will influence governments to observe the right to a fair and public trial.

The International Commission of Jurists has proposed draft principles on the independence of the judiciary and lawyers to the United Nations for study and eventual action. The proposal insists that an independent legal profession is "an essential condition for the respect and protection of human rights under the rule of law." The statement goes on to assert that the lawyer "is not .. to be identified by the authorities or the public with his client or his client's cause, however popular or unpopular it may be." Human rights can only be secured when the administration of justice is independent of the executive and legislative branches of government in every nation.

OTHER NONGOVERNMENTAL ORGANIZATIONS

One of the most venerable organizations devoted to international human rights is the International League for Human Rights founded by Roger Baldwin. Originally called the International League for the Rights of Man, this group has been obscured a bit by a plethora of new groups. But the International League continues to send missions to troubled nations such as Chile, testifies regularly before Congress, and encourages its affiliates and correspondents all around the world. The league has consultative status with the United Nations, the UN Educational, Scientific, and Cultural Organization UNESCO, the International Labor Organization, and the Council of Europe.

Other well-established and highly regarded human rights groups include Freedom House, which each year issues a map of the world with each nation color coded according to the degree of freedom its people have. The level of freedom does not rise constantly each year, because Freedom House reminds us regularly, only a minority of the 160 nations of the world have democratic institutions compatible with the human rights promises of the UN covenants.

Newer American rights groups include the Lawyers Committee for Human Rights, Americas Watch, Helsinki Watch, and Asia Watch. Inspired to some extent by the enactment of Section 502B by Congress in 1974 these ambitious and resourceful new groups send observers to troubled countries, publish scores of studies, testify before Congress, write scores of editorials, and prepare critical studies on the limitations and weaknesses of the State Department annual reports.

LIMITS ON THE EFFECTIVENESS OF NONGOVERNMENTAL ORGANIZATIONS

The emergence of private groups dedicated to non-ideological issues has characterized the present age. The environmentalists seemed to burst onto the scene with the first Earth Day in 1970. Peace activists began in the 1950s to bring about a ban on nuclear testing in the atmosphere. Groups such as Physicians for Social Responsibility, the Union of Concerned Scientists, and the Lawyers Alliance for Nuclear Arms Control continue to grow in numbers and influence. Private groups such as Bread for the World have increased public awareness of world hunger. Bob Geldof, the gangly British rock star, created the Live Aid concert in July 1985 that raised more than $100 million for the hungry in Africa.

Sometimes it seems that people and private organizations with a moral vision can do more than governments, which are paralyzed by their bureaucracies. Nongovernmental human rights groups aspire to educate and change and inspire. But they need a strong and ever-improving corpus of national and international law that defines and enforces human rights. Private action, however compelling, has its limits. It can change the atmosphere but new laws are required to change the structure. Martin Luther King, Jr., changed the national climate in America. But it was the Civil Rights Acts of 1964 and the Voting Rights Act of 1965 that changed forever the legal status of blacks in America.

Leaders cannot succeed without followers. And followers must be more than docile; they have to inspire leaders to lead. One is tempted to think that in the end private groups are more important for the advancement of human rights than governments are. Governments will not generally rebuke other governments. Politicians are more concerned about financial benefits for their own nation than about the state of human rights in another friendly or unfriendly nation. Hence it will be people like the abolitionists in America in the early 1800s or the followers of Gandhi who practiced passive resistance in India, who will make the world pay heed to human rights.

An international criminal commission will not work without an army of private attorneys general. But armies of private protectors of human rights cannot bring about the rule of law without attorneys, courts, and prosecutors. Law and morality are inseparable. Perhaps Abraham Lincoln said it best: "Let reverence for the laws . . . become the political religion of the nation."

STANDARDS OF MEASUREMENT FOR HUMAN RIGHTS

Underlying and complicating the mission of the governmental and nongovernmental human rights agencies is the emerging question of a scientific methodology for measuring and monitoring the observance of human rights. An abundance of data is increasingly available from the International Labor Organization and the World Health Organization on the state of health, food, education, and housing in all nations. Is it possible to transfer or adapt the techniques used to measure socioeconomic rights to civil and political rights?

There is a growing and deepening feeling in the international human rights community that reporting on human rights is too often a haphazard enterprise. The November 1986 issue of *Human Rights Quarterly* is devoted entirely to this subject. The problems are clear. There is too little standardized, uniform, and universally accepted information on human rights. There is as yet no standard protocol for reporting on abuses of human rights nor is there a central repository for reports of violations. The nearest thing to such a central source of information about human rights is Internet, a privately financed agency now housed at the Harvard Law School, which has collected and collated an amazing array of studies about human rights everywhere in the world.

Efforts toward standardization of procedures for assessing the state of human rights are probably more advanced in Latin America than anywhere else. The Inter-American Institute for Human Rights in San Jose, Costa Rica, has produced guidelines and training for human rights agencies in Central America. Americas Watch and Washington Office on Latin America, a church-related human rights group, have organized seminars to examine methodological issues. Freedom House has developed a seven-point freedom scale to grade and rank nations. The annual "Country Reports" of the U.S. State Department sometimes cross-reference their findings with those of private human rights groups. The 1985 State Department report included for the first time an appendix listing selected violations of human rights. The American Association for the Advancement of Science has organized symposia on measuring human rights performances.

Despite all these burgeoning efforts, reporting on human rights is still sometimes haphazard, episodic, and subjective. The first and crucial question is of course, Who supplies the information? If the government itself is the source, there is automatic suspicion. If a United Nations agency supplies the information, it is again suspect if the information comes from an individual government directly. Data from human rights groups must be assessed in light of the ideological orientation of the group. Amnesty International has sought to be free of ideological bias, whether left, right, or center. But some governments who do not fare well in Amnesty International's annual volume complain that they were required by morality and by law to act against dangerously subversive persons and groups. And it is the alleged presence of enemies of the state that makes accurate reporting on human rights a complex matter. Governments that violate the human rights of their citizens almost always claim that terrorists or revolutionaries within their borders make such conduct necessary. The military junta in Argentina from 1976 to 1983 labeled the Monteneros subversives, traitors, or Communists. President Duarte in El Salvador, like the Reagan administration, calls the insurgents in his country terrorists and Marxists-Leninists. Chile's President Pinochet stigmatizes all his political opponents—from left to right—as subversives and Communists.

Under the Marcos regime in the Philippines the insurgents or rebels were labeled Communists, although there is little evidence that, after the defeat of the Mao-assisted Huks in the 1950s, the New People's Army (NPA) received assistance from Communist sources outside the Philippines. But the allegation that the NPA is a Communist group has persisted in the world press long after the disappearance of the Marcos regime.

An evaluation of the state of human rights in any country must therefore include some evaluation of the government's claim that it had to use force to combat a subversive enemy and that violations of human rights were required for the protection of the human rights of the vast majority of citizens. Human rights groups have tended to skirt that political and ideological thicket by simply reporting violations of human rights as they occur. Private human rights groups, following the lead of Amnesty International, have tended to report on assaults on human rights by nongovernmental groups. But this clearly infuriates governments in power, who claim that the violations of human rights with which they are charged are done for the highest of motives and in order to protect their citizens from the violence of a revolutionary insurgency.

The adoption of a uniform methodology to measure human rights violations would be greatly strengthened by the creation of a United Nations high commissioner for human rights. That office could coordinate the collection of information about the state of human rights in the world, collaborate with private human interest groups, and assist in developing scientific methods of measurement. In the words of the Universal Declaration of Human Rights, there would then be a "common standard of achievement for all peoples and all nations."

IV. THE HOPE OF THE HUMAN RIGHTS REVOLUTION

13. A Permanent International Court

The human rights movement must sooner or later confront this question: Should the violation of international human rights be criminalized? In any system of law certain injuries are made compensable by fines levied by the state or by money damages to the victims. Sometimes both remedies are made available. But some injuries are so serious that they are made into crimes. Should the nations of the world declare certain egregious violations of human rights to be criminal acts? The concept of the international criminalization of violations of human rights was born really for the first time at Nuremberg. It was hoped in 1946 that the Nuremberg trials would flower into a permanent international criminal commission. That dream has not yet materialized, but the Nuremberg trials provide a precedent and a model for such a court.

THE NUREMBERG TRIALS

On January 13, 1942, the United States and its nine European allies made it clear to the world in the Declaration of St. James's Palace, addressed to their military opponents, that "there will be punishment of those guilty or responsible for the crimes, whether they have ordered them, perpetrated them or participated in them." The Allies wished to prevent a repeat of the past. When the Germans signed the Treaty of Versailles in 1920 they agreed to hand over to the Allied military tribunal some nine hundred persons accused of violations of the laws of war but never fulfilled this promise. This time the Allies wished to make it clear that war crimes would not go unpunished. What the Nazis and the Japanese were doing surely violated international law. It transgressed the Kellogg-Briand pact of 1928, which removed war as an instrument of national policy although it did not prescribe any specific punishment for those who violated the pact.

The Allied powers chose the medieval city of Nuremberg for the solemn conclave devoted to punishing those who violated human rights guaranteed by international law. Ironically Nuremberg was the scene for party rallies at which Nazi leaders strutted and ranted, the birthplace of Der Stuermer with its racist diatribes, and the city where Herman Goering, the president of the Reichstag, first proclaimed the anti-Jewish laws that came to be called the Nuremberg Laws.

Arranged together at Nuremberg were the legal forces of the United States, the USSR, Great Britain, and France. The self-evident limitation of the tribunal was that it was made up of the victors sitting in judgment on the vanquished. Justice Robert Jackson, who had taken leave from the United States Supreme Court to act as the prosecutor at Nuremberg, gave the only possible explanation of the situation by stating that "the worldwide scope of the new aggression carried out by these men has left but few real neutrals. Either the victors must judge the vanquished or we must leave the defeated to judge themselves. After the first world war we learned the futility of the latter course."

In his opening address to the Nuremberg tribunal Justice Jackson also took on the anticipated defense of the Nazi officials— that they were required to obey the orders of their superiors and that therefore they could not be held liable. To this Justice Jackson replied: "The United Nations charter recognizes that one who has committed criminal acts may not take refuge in superior orders . . . nor in the doctrine that his crimes were acts of state. These twin principles working together have heretofore resulted in immunity for . . . those [guilty of] . . . the great crimes of peace and humanity."

The other prosecutors at Nuremberg agreed with Justice Jackson's conclusion. Chief British Prosecutor Sir Hartley Shawcross stated that "there is no immunity for those who obey orders which are manifestly contrary to the very law of nature from which international law has grown." Chief Soviet Prosecutor Roman Rudenko agreed: "Execution of an obviously criminal order does not exonerate one from criminal responsibility."

But Justice Jackson did acknowledge that in some rare circumstances a soldier may *not* be held accountable for carrying out orders. In the *Farber* decision Justice Jackson declared that "an order is a complete defense where it is given under such circumstances as to afford the one receiving it no other moral choice than to comply therewith." A soldier told to shoot in a firing squad is not chargeable, Justice Jackson said, with the death of a person "even if such death was unjust."

Two moral and legal principles that previously were not generally accepted as a part of international law became law at Nuremberg: The orders of a superior do not justify transgressions against human rights although they may mitigate the punishment. Individuals as well as governments may be held accountable for war crimes. Today these principles are by general agreement a part of customary international law. The Nuremberg principles were endorsed by the United Nations General Assembly a few months after the conclusion of the Nuremberg and Tokyo trials.

Article 6(c) of the Nuremberg charter may contain the most enduring achievement of the entire Nuremberg process. It outlaws crimes against humanity (a concept invented at Nuremberg) even when committed by a state against its own subjects and "whether or not in violation of the domestic law where perpetrated." This is irreconcilable on its face with the classical doctrine of sovereignty. It qualifies that doctrine in the name of the concept that there are certain acts no nation may tolerate because they are "crimes against humanity."

The Nuremberg trials lasted 10 months, with 216 days of trial. There were 33 witnesses for the prosecution and 204 witnesses for the defense. The best lawyers in Germany represented the twenty-one indicted Nazis—at Allied expense. Those indicted included Herman Goering, the founder of the Gestapo and Hitler's heir apparent, Joachim von Ribbentrop, foreign minister, and Rudof Hess, once deputy leader of Germany, who feigned amnesia and then admitted it was a sham and later, ironically, became amnesiac and paranoid at the trial.

The entire cabinet and the top military leaders where charged with a wide range of heinous crimes. The evidence against them was staggering. The Nazis were convicted out of their own mouths and by their own memos. Films of thousands of dead bodies, taken by the Allied forces immediately after the concentration camps fell into their hands, were made a part of the four thousand documents submitted. The horrors of the Third Reich were made plain for all time. Lampshades made of human skin were but one of the exhibits that revealed the moral anesthetization of the German people. The Nuremberg record contains proof beyond doubt that the Nazis exterminated at least six million Jews. Other atrocities, such as the extermination of thousands of people in asylums, are recorded forever in the twenty-two volumes of the proceedings of the Nuremberg trial.

Sentence was pronounced on October 1, 1946, and early on the morning of October 16, 1946, the death sentences were carried out; the bodies were cremated in secrecy lest a cult arise.

Although the hope of the architects of Nuremberg was that it would be the forerunner of a permanent international tribunal for those who violate international law, the initial energy and enthusiasm faded away quickly. The second-echelon war criminals had trials in the four zones of military occupation. Of the 185 defendants 13 received the death penalty, and 85 were imprisoned, 8 of them for life. But thereafter the Allied powers lost their drive to see justice done to all who planned and engineered the Nazi conspiracy.

EFFORTS TO ESTABLISH AN INTERNATIONAL CRIMINAL COURT

The aspirations that helped to create the Nuremberg tribunal were not entirely new in the world. In 1920 the Advisory Committee of Jurists was set up by the League of Nations to plan the establishment of the Permanent Court of International Justice. This group was formed after the failure to use a provision of the Treaty of Versailles to try the German ex-emperor "for a supreme offense against international morality and the sanctity of treaties."

When the League of Nations rejected a resolution to establish an international criminal court, the International Law Association, a private organization of jurists and professors, subjected the idea of an international criminal court to intensive study. A draft statute for an international criminal court was accepted by the association in 1928. In 1937 an international conference of jurists and lawyers convened at Geneva and produced two conventions—one for the prevention and punishment of terrorism, the other for the creation of an international court. The outbreak of World War II eclipsed these efforts to establish an international court.

After the Nuremberg tribunal was dismantled the General Assembly of the United Nations invited the International Law Commission, a private organization, to investigate the desirability and feasibility of creating an international criminal court. The commission concluded that such a court was desirable and possible. In 1951 and again in 1953 the General Assembly appointed two successive committees to produce a draft statute for an international criminal court. In 1954 the General Assembly concluded that the draft code of offenses against the peace and security of humankind be deferred until the United Nations had finalized its deliberations on the nature of aggression. Although the United Nations finally adopted a definition of aggression in 1974, no further progress has been made to revive and advance the efforts to create an international criminal court.

The absence of an international criminal court to try and punish crimes against humanity has brought about anomalous situations like the trial of Adolph Eichmann in Israel. The abduction of Eichmann from Argentina by Israel was arguably contrary to well-settled rules of international law. The trial and execution of Eichmann pursuant to laws enacted after the time of Eichmann's admittedly deplorable crimes raises problems of law and justice. The dangers of nations engaging in self-help and acting as vigilantes are self-evident.

In the absence of an international criminal tribunal a few nations have followed the example of Israel's Nazi collaborators law. This law, enacted by the Knesset in 1950, makes crimes against the Jewish people, crimes against humanity, and war crimes a part of Israel's criminal law. In 1952 Holland criminalized breaches of the law of warfare, inhumane treatment, and systematic terrorizing of civilians in time of war. The criminal codes of Hungary, Poland, Yugoslavia, and the Soviet Union have comparable provisions.

The list of crimes defined by customary international law or by conventions among nations as punishable by any or all nations is growing. The list harkens back to the venerable tradition of referring to *delicta jure gentium,* or offenses against the law of nations or peoples. In addition to slave trading and piracy, crimes against the law of nations include drug trafficking, counterfeiting currency, airline hijacking, and war crimes.

The usefulness of an international criminal court is self-evident. If such a tribunal existed it might be a way to inhibit terrorists like Idi Amin and Colonel Kaddafi. An international court would at least confine such leaders to their own countries, since they would be vulnerable to prosecution anywhere outside their country's borders. Such a status would help to erode domestic support as well as international relations with such despots. It would also have been helpful during the dark years from 1976 to 1983 when an authoritarian military government terrorized the people of Argentina. After the return of democracy to Argentina several of these leaders were punished by a special court established by President Raul Alphonsin. But if the military leaders of Argentina had known before and during their reign of terror that they would be held accountable to an international court, their conduct would in all probability have been more restrained.

The same thing could be said about the regime of President Ferdinand Marcos in the Philippines or the dictatorship of President Augusto Pinochet in Chile. And if the leaders of South Africa knew that they could be tried during or after their tenure in office for crimes against humanity, their conduct would almost certainly be more moderate.

Since crimes against the 1948 Geneva conventions on the rules of war are now at least a part of customary international law, an international criminal court could hear petitions that nations at war were in violation of specific provisions of those treaties. Complaints against the conduct of Americans in Vietnam could have been referred to the international tribunal rather than to the unsatisfactory United States military tribunal that tried and convicted Lt. William Calley. An international criminal commission could hear the allegations of human rights abuses in the Iran-Iraq war, in the Middle East, or in El Salvador and Nicaragua.

In the extensive literature on the subject most experts agree that establishing a tribunal to adjudicate criminal violations of human rights must be the next step in the development of international human rights laws. Some jurists might hold that the very idea of an international criminal court infringes on the sovereignty of nations. But that position has been undercut and even destroyed by the Nuremberg tribunal, which clearly held that individuals as well as nations can be held accountable for offenses that contravene certain basic moral norms known or knowable by all human beings.

Article 6(c) of the Nuremberg charter defines crimes against humanity as "murder, extermination, enslavement, deportation, and other inhuman acts committed against any civilian population before or during the war, or prosecutions on political, racial or religious grounds . . . whether or not in violation of the domestic law of the country where perpetrated." The Nuremberg tribunal asserted the superiority of international law over national law in these terms: "The very essence of the charter is that individuals have international duties which transcend the national obligations of obedience imposed by the individual state. He who violates the laws of war cannot obtain immunity while acting in pursuance of the authority of the state, if the state in authorizing action moves outside its competence under international law."

OBSTACLES TO AN INTERNATIONAL COURT

Despite the fact that the United Nations and the Nuremberg tribunal internationalized certain crimes, United States hostility to the international criminal court began early in the 1950s. A debate on the issue in the *American Bar Association Journal* in 1952 set the stage for opposition by the American Bar Association. Opponents claimed that the proposed international court would reduce the safeguards United States law already provided for Americans indicted and tried for crime. Those opposed to the international criminal court argued that the holdings of Nuremberg were intended to apply only to wartime and that the United States had no need for the proposed international court because the United States had its own code of military justice for offenses committed during a war. The neo-isolationism of the 1950s and the conservative, even reactionary, character of the American Bar Association during that period continued to assure the opposition of America's lawyers to any consideration of an international criminal court. That attitude persisted until the late 1970s when the American Bar Association urged the ratification of all the major human rights treaties. No proposal to enter into an international criminal court has ever been made by any administration or by the Senate. It seems fair to state that the United States, the prime mover for the establishment of the United Nations, became by its inaction the prime opponent of the proposed 1951 UN draft for an international criminal court.

The United States also diluted or defeated support for an international criminal court by refusing to accept the decision of the International Court of Justice at The Hague in favor of Nicaragua, which had sued the United States for mining the harbors of Nicaragua. In 1984 the World Court ruled fifteen to one that the United States was bound to accept its jurisdiction. On June 27, 1986, the World Court, ruling on its merits, held that all United States military aid to the contras violated international law because, through the use of force, it interfered with the internal affairs of a sovereign nation. The United States was reminded that it had ratified Article 94 of the UN charter, which requires the signatories "to comply with the decisions of the International Court of Justice in any case in which it is a party." The World Court rejected the argument that the United States acted in collective self-defense in helping the contras and held that the United States was "under a duty immediately to cease and refrain from all such acts." When Nicaragua subsequently took its claim for damages to the UN Security Council, the United States defeated a claim by exercising its right to veto.

Although some lawyers may justify the legal maneuvers of the United States State Department in defeating the claims of Nicaragua, the clear consensus among international lawyers is that the United States trampled upon the spirit and even the letter of international law in defying the International Court of Justice. The ICJ was founded as the legal arm of the United Nations. It has served in that capacity in a low-key manner. There has always been some hope of expanding the ICJ's authority to include important issues not now in its jurisdiction, such as quasi-criminal or even criminal issues. But by its resistance to the World Court from 1984 to 1986, the United States has stifled whatever hope the jurists had for a greater utilization of the ICJ.

How would a truly effective international criminal court operate? Would the UN General Assembly, acting as grand jury, indict persons or nations? Or could a group of regional or worldwide prosecuting attorneys be appointed or elected? What rules of evidence would be utilized? Would there be a guarantee of a trial by jury? If so, from what countries would the jurors be chosen? Would the death penalty be imposed or would it be banned?

These issues may seem insurmountable. But they are less awesome than the creation of the United Nations. If 160 nations found it possible to yield a part of their sovereignty to join that world body, they might well be prepared to agree to a tribunal that would do what domestic criminal laws everywhere do—punish lawless conduct with swift and effective sanctions. A system of international punishments and sanctions against the Stalins and Hitlers of this world would predictably act as a deterrent in the same way that local, state, and federal punishments for antisocial conduct deter crime in America. It could be argued that in a world ever more closely linked by commercial, economic, and cultural contacts, the threat that a regime could be adjudicated to be outlaws would have such an enormous impact on the economy and the morale of a country that its rulers would be strongly constrained not to violate international law.

A HIGH COMMISSIONER FOR HUMAN RIGHTS

In 1949 the United Nations General Assembly created the office of UN high commissioner for refugees; the vote was 35 to 7, with 13 abstentions. The UN high commissioner for refugees oversees the application of the various international instruments relating to refugees, including questions of asylum, and attends to the growing problem of displaced persons. By everyone's admission the UN high commissioner for refugees has done extraordinary work—as symbolized by the Nobel Peace Prize awarded to this office. In 1950 Uruguay proposed to the General Assembly that a UN office of high commissioner or attorney general for human rights be created. This was urged as a possible compromise resolution of the dispute concerning the right of individual petition under the draft covenant on civil and political rights. Individual petitions, Uruguay argued, would not be permitted in the bodies to be created to implement the forthcoming treaties on human rights, but these would be allowed by an attorney general for the world who would report on threats to human rights and alert every available local body that could offer a remedy.

The idea for a high commissioner for human rights originated with Rene Cassin, one of the authors of the Universal Declaration of Human Rights. Professor Cassin's original proposal contemplated a rather elaborate two-tier system by which the aggrieved person could appeal to the UN Commission on Human Rights and, if unsuccessful there, to a universal court of human rights. This proposal, offered at the UN by France, failed to gain much support. But the idea of some form of attorney general or high commissioner for human rights has intrigued the United Nations since its inception. The excellent book by Roger Stenson Clark, *A United Nations High Commissioner for Human Rights,* published in 1972, is filled with evidence of the fascination the majority of the members of the United Nations have always shared for a high commissioner for human rights.

The term *high commissioner* was first used by the League of Nations. It faintly suggests certain apsects of British colonialism. In the 1960s some urged that the title of rapporteur or special rapporteur would be less likely to scare off governments than the lofty title of high commissioner, but misgivings about the name have not been raised publicly since that time. The term has probably been retained because it would identify the proposed high commissioner for human rights with the continuous and almost spectacular successes of the UN high commissioner for refugees.

Over the years every version of the high commissioner for human rights has stipulated that he or she would report on the violations of human rights around the world to the General Assembly, offer his or her good offices for the resolution of disputes, urge the allegedly offending governments to comply with UN standards, and in general assist all nations to carry out their duties under Articles 55 and 56 of the UN charter. Objections that the proposal was overambitious have been one of the reasons why the Cassin and Uruguay proposals did not receive majority support within the United Nations in the 1950s.

Efforts by the State Department to have President Kennedy endorse the idea of a high commissioner for human rights were not completely successful, but on September 20, 1963, the president did tell the UN General Assembly that the United States would cooperate with efforts to create more efficient procedures to enforce internationally recognized human rights; he expressed United States opposition to "apartheid and all forms of human oppression" and went on to proclaim that "new efforts are needed if this Assembly's Declaration of Human Rights, now fifteen years old, is to have full meaning."

In 1964, at meetings in Paris and Geneva, all the major nongovernmental organizations issued a joint statement in favor of a high commissioner for human rights. Early in 1965 Costa Rica introduced a proposal for a high commissioner as part of the UN Commission on Human Rights. The main objections to the proposal came from the Soviet representative to the UN Commission on Human Rights; he felt that the contents of the proposal were already on the agenda of the General Assembly. Due to the objections of the USSR and some Arab nations, the debate over the proposal for a high commissioner for human rights was not resolved in 1965.

In 1966 fifteen nongovernmental organizations issued a statement supporting the Costa Rican draft while acknowledging that the functions proposed fell short of what the NGOs would have liked. Later in 1966 a working group appointed by the UN Commission on Human Rights produced a thorough document analyzing the role of the proposed high commissioner for human rights. It supported the concept of a single individual as high commissioner rather than the collegiate body proposed by a minority of the working group. Those favoring a collegiate body pointed to the International Labor Organization and made the argument that a collegiate body would run less risk of error than a single person and, because it would represent many cultures and diverse legal systems, would be more acceptable to various nations.

The high commissioner for human rights would be mandated to promote and encourage universal and effective respect for human rights but would have little, if any, power to enforce compliance by recalcitrant public officials. The office would not collide with the clear guarantee in Article 2 of the UN charter that "nothing contained in the present Charter shall authorize the

United Nations to intervene in matters which are essentially within the domestic jurisdiction of any state."

Despite the restricted role to be assigned to the high commissioner for human rights in every version of the proposed office, the Soviet Union has persistently claimed that human rights are not the subject of international law. This position contradicts the Soviet acquiescence to the principles of Nuremberg and acceptance of the UN conventions on civil and political rights. The point insisted upon by Soviet spokespersons is not taken seriously by scholars of international law since there is now a substantial body of law and practice concerning individuals as the subjects of international law.

One function the high commissioner would clearly be required to perform would be a thorough global survey of the state of each human right in each nation of the world. The UN Commission on Human Rights has attempted to perform that function, but for a wide variety of reasons it has not done so effectively. The absence of a comprehensive and credible yearbook on the state of human rights prompted Amnesty International to start such a survey several years ago. Its annual report is highly regarded, but it cannot expect to have the credibility of a well-documented report from a UN agency. The absence of a universally accepted annual report on human rights by a public international agency prompted the United States Congress in the mid-1970s to require the State Department to produce such an annual. Although that document has had an extraordinary impact, it is still open to the charge that it emphasizes events and data that support the ideological assumptions of the administration in power.

The mere publication of information about human rights in various countries is likely to produce salutary results. Even South Africa has anxieties about what the world thinks of its practice of apartheid. It is not content to be a pariah nation. It fights back with allegations that it is in the process of developing a dual but equal existence for blacks and whites in South Africa. Morris Abram identified this phenomenon in *Foreign Affairs* magazine in 1969: "Despite the harsh realities of our politics world opinion *is* a force to be reckoned with. Governments do devote much time and energy, both in and out of the United Nations, to defending and embellishing their own human rights image."

In late 1967 the UN Commission on Human Rights gave its full endorsement to the working group's recommendations for the office of commissioner by a vote of 20 to 7, with 2 abstentions. Nations approving included Great Britain, the United States, Israel, and several Third World countries. Opposed were India, the United Arab Republic, and the USSR. France abstained. Observers attribute Arab support for the Soviet position to the problems the Arab bloc has with Israel. Soviet opposition centered on the fact that in 1966 the United Nations had finally adopted the two covenants on economic and political rights and that as a result the office of high commissioner would not be necessary. The Soviet spokesman also claimed that the International Court of Justice was authorized to perform some of the tasks to be assigned to the high commissioner for human rights. The concept of a single high commissioner also posed problems, the Soviets asserted, because he or she would be responsive only to the legal system of his own country or region; the advisory committee designed to meet his objection was, for the representative of the Soviet Union, inadequate and unworkable.

On June 6, 1967 the Economic and Social Council of the United Nations (ECOSOC), which recommends human rights legislation for the General Assembly, approved the establishment of a high commissioner for human rights. During the debates on the issue of the high commissioner in the General Assembly, Japan recorded its change of position from one of questioning to one of approval. France changed its position to one of firm support. India also appeared to soften its previous opposition to the idea. But the Soviet Union continued its opposition, threatening a boycott of the office if it were created. In the face of this controversy the General Assembly postponed the resolution. But it appears that eighty to one hundred nations would approve the creation of the office of high commissioner for human rights, while about twenty nations are strongly opposed.

The proposal for a UN high commissioner for human rights came to the floor of the General Assembly once again in 1977. It was assumed that the proposal would finally pass, since Western diplomats had secured the support of the Third World. The proposal made reference to issues of concern to developing nations, and the office of high commissioner had been unofficially promised to a person from an African country. The sponsors were confident that, nearly thirty years after Uruguay first sponsored the idea, the General Assembly would act favorably. The support of President Carter was deemed significant.

The sponsors were so sure of passage that they declined to accept a modification that would have diluted the proposal by diminishing the powers of the office of high commissioner. There was therefore surprise and disappointment when a motion by Cuba to table the proposal was successful. The rejection was unusual because by long tradition in the United Nations carefully planned motions are almost always agreed to. Behind the alternative proposal offered by Cuba was a movement to reaffirm the ideal, long cherished by the Third World, of the indivisibility of economic and political human rights. Those who objected to the appointment of the high commissioner were implicitly putting forward the new international machinery designed largely to protect the political rights so precious to the West. In essence the substitute motion offered was an effort to undo the bifurcation of human rights into civil and political rights on the one hand and economic and cultural rights on the other. That separation, agreed to in the 1950s by the Western powers, was challenged in the 1960s by those involved in the decolonization movement. Hence the defeat of the proposed high commissioner for human rights was in a certain sense a turning point with respect to the way in which the United Nations approaches human rights. Western nations now continue to say in essence that it is not feasible for the United Nations to deal with the complex issues of international economics. But the Third World will continue to insist on linking political and economic rights. The division between the developed and developing nations on this issue is deep and at the moment apparently irreconcilable. So long as this is the case it may not be possible for the proposal for a high commissioner for human rights to become a reality.

But the idea of a high commissioner for human rights continues to attract broad support. The Reagan administration approved of the idea on December 10, 1982. Michael Novak, the United States representative on the UN Commission on Human Rights, testified before Congress that the permanent presence of a high commissioner devoted to human rights would bring "higher visibility and prestige" to the issue. He also asserted that in 1981 there had been "good progress in the ideal of a UN high commissioner on human rights." But he was cautious about the creation of the office because of anticipated budgetary difficulties within the United Nations. Reflecting the almost obsessional fear of communism within his administration, Novak also warned of what he conceived to be "the danger of this office falling into the hands of those whose conception of human rights, and practice of human rights, are far different from those of Western ideals."

On March 10, 1983, the United Nations Human Rights Commission adopted an essentially procedural resolution on a high commissioner for human rights by a vote of 24 to 11 with 7 abstentions. The United States voted in favor of the resolution. In similar action in 1983 the UN Subcommission on the Prevention of Discrimination and Protection of Minorities voted on terms of reference for the mandate of the high commissioner. The high commissioner would be elected directly by the General Assembly for a five-year term, he or she would not serve for two consecutive terms, and he or she should be elected on the principle of regional rotation.

Those who wonder whether the United Nations General Assembly will ever approve the office of high commissioner for human rights should recall that few observers in 1966 would have predicted that, after twelve years of sporadic debate, the United Nations would adopt the human rights covenants. Strong intellectual and moral forces operating on behalf of human rights may make the acceptance of some international machinery to enforce human rights virtually inevitable.

14. The Right to Food

The emergence of the law related to political rights wins applause whenever and wherever jurists and diplomats from the West come together. But the representatives of underdeveloped nations have far different concerns. For these countries hunger and homelessness are far more pressing than torture and detention for political reasons.

The sharp separation of the priorities of the rich and the poor nations is nowhere more evident than in the debates in the United Nations General Assembly where the one hundred nations of the Third World regularly press their demands for a new international economic order. Jurists, diplomats, and even human rights activists from the nations whose economies tend to dominate the world do not think in terms of guaranteeing the right to food, shelter, and literacy. Former colonies understandably feel antipathy toward the traditions of nations such as England, France, Belgium, Spain, Portugal, and Holland, which grew rich by exploiting the natural resources of their colonies. When the onetime colonial powers expound on the glories of the political liberties they often denied to their former colonial subjects, those new nations who fought their way to freedom cannot be expected to be impressed or edified.

The rivalry between those who seek to give priority to political and social rights and those who emphasize economic rights is reflected in the separate UN covenants for these categories of human rights. While this dualism may be unavoidable, though tragic, the developed nations in their self-righteous emphasis on and exaltation of political rights, give the appearance of callousness towards a world that cries out for food, fuel, and fertilizer.

The facts about the underdeveloped nations are grim and sobering. In the summer of 1986 the fifth billion person on the globe was born. In all probability he or she came to life in the Third World, where over 80 percent of the world's children are born. Fifty percent of the world's hungry live in just five countries: India, Bangladesh, Nigeria, Pakistan, and Indonesia. Africa, the poorest continent, is a special and tragic case. The per capita food production in Africa has slipped 20 percent over the past twenty-five years. The Food and Agricultural Organization (FAO) estimates that Africa's capacity to produce food could decline by another 30 percent in the next twenty-five years. In Africa the level of food imports rose from $2 billion in 1970 to $10 billion in 1980.

For more than a generation the nonaligned nations of the Third World have been arguing—sometimes imperiously—that fundamental equality for all human beings, the basis for all human rights guarantees, can be achieved only by first furnishing an adequate diet to all people on earth. No one would openly contradict this proposition. But the developed nations have not responded to its stark appeal. Even the nations that promptly and enthusiastically ratified the majestic United Nations covenants have not always been conspicuous for their zeal in extending themselves to fulfill the promise of those treaties. The promises are clear. Article 25 of the UN Universal Declaration of Human Rights, agreed to by member nations on December 10, 1948, states that everyone has "the right to a standard of living adequate for the health and well-being of himself and his family, including food." Article 11 of the UN International Covenant on Economic, Social, and Cultural Rights recognizes the "right of everyone . . . to . . . adequate food, clothing and housing." The rights recognized also include the "continuous improvement of living conditions."

Signatory nations commit themselves to "take appropriate steps to ensure the realization" of these rights both "individually and through international cooperation." The commitments are quite specific. Nations promise to "improve methods of production, conservation and distribution of food making full use of technical and scientific knowledge, by disseminating knowledge of the principles of nutrition and by developing or reforming agrarian systems in such a way as to achieve the most efficient development and utilization of natural resources." Similar promises are made by all signatory nations to reduce infant mortality, provide for the "healthy development" of children, prevent "epidemic, endemic, occupational and other diseases" and create conditions that would assure medical attention to all requiring it. Comparable pledges to education are included in Article 13. The creation of primary schools for all children is a promise and not merely an ideal.

Human rights activists in the developing nations obviously have a greater affinity for the economic rights mandated in the UN covenants than do their counterparts in the developed nations. And clearly the present state of those economic rights can bring dissatisfaction, even despair, to those countries that daily experience a violation of those economic rights the family of nations pledged to implement. Those rights are now a part of customary international law, binding on nations—at least on those that formally ratified these treaties.

The violation of these rights is an appalling spectacle. Hunger and illiteracy plague the world. It is not certain that these twin perils are being eradicated. They may be even more present when by the year 2000 world population rises to 6.2 billion human beings. The problem of world hunger, by almost everyone's estimation, is not due to a shortage of food but to the maldistribution of food. Each day the world produces two pounds of grain for each person on Earth. This is enough to furnish three thousand calories for everyone each day. But from 340 million to 900 million persons are chronically malnourished. One-sixth of the people in the eighty-seven developing countries will have chronic and serious health problems as a result of an inadequate diet.

The worldwide neglect of the internationally recognized right to food can be seen in the following horrendous statistics:

1. Every sixty seconds twenty-eight people die from hunger-related causes.
2. One child in ten dies before its first birthday.
3. In eighty-three poor countries 3 percent of the landowners control 80 percent of the land.
4. Seventy percent of the world's people have only 10 percent of the world's resources available to them.
5. Fifty percent of the world's people lack clean drinking water.
6. The developing nations now owe over $800 billion—two-thirds of it to lending institutions in the United States.

Under the American Convention on Human Rights, subscribed to and ratified by the majority of nations in Latin America, the right to food is guaranteed to the 400 million inhabitants of that continent. But the economic situation in Latin America does not reflect what the American Convention on Human Rights promised.

Latin America is one of the world's richest and most fertile regions. It has more arable land than any other continent. It has 16 percent of the world's cultivatable land with only 6 percent of the world's population. But every fifth person in Latin America is a victim of severe malnutrition. One of the basic reasons is the need for land reform. In Latin America 7 percent of the people control 93.8 percent of the land. One-half of the land in Central America is used not to produce food for the 24 million people in the five nations of that region but to produce crops and cattle for export. Similarly Brazil, one of the world's largest exporters, has more acreage under cultivation than the United States, but 70 percent of the population suffers some degree of malnutrition. The debt of $360 billion owed by Latin America will continue to prompt the leaders of that continent to encourage production of cash crops for export rather than food staples for the local population.

The Presidential Commission on World Hunger, chaired by Sol M. Linowitz, recommended in 1980 that the United States government "make the elimination of hunger the primary focus of its relationships with the developing countries." In its report the commission offered evidence for its conclusion that "it would be possible to eliminate the worst aspects of hunger and malnutrition by the year 2000."

The moral position of the commission on the right to food is strongly worded:

Whether one speaks of human rights or basic human needs, the right to food is the most basic of all. Unless that right is first fulfilled, the protection of other human rights becomes a mockery for those who must spend all their energy merely to maintain life itself. The correct moral and ethical position on hunger is beyond debate. The world's major religions and philosophical systems share two universal values: respect for human dignity and a sense of social justice. Hunger is the ultimate affront to both.

The commission termed hunger "the central strand in the web of underdevelopment— poverty, powerlessness, low productivity, lack of education, unemployment, disease, and high rates of population growth."

The corollary of this firm position is that the United States "by concentrating its international efforts on the elimination of hunger . . . would provide the strongest possible demonstration of its renewed dedication to the cause of human rights." Further, an effective campaign against world hunger "holds the key to both global and national security" because it will help to "break the impasse in 'North-South' relations." The commission noted that an emphasis on the right to food in United States foreign policy would also benefit American farmers. In 1980 American farmers exported two-thirds of their wheat, about half of their rice and soybeans, and about one-quarter of their corn. The hundreds of thousands of arable acres deliberately kept out of production could, if utilized, make America "the breadbasket of the world."

The Presidential Commission on World Hunger summarized the bleak picture humanity confronts in the years ahead. It cited predictions by the World Bank that some 470 million of the world's people will still be living in absolute poverty in the year 2000. By that time nearly eight out of ten people will live in the developing world. The commission offered some creative ideas. One was that the person within the federal government in charge of economic assistance to foreign nations be accorded cabinet-level status and that Congress undertake a complete revision of the Food for Peace Program (public law 480).

Although the mandate of the Presidential Commission on World Hunger did not extend to an evaluation of overall priorities of the United States government, it did comment that the vast sum spent by the United States and other nations on arms and armies (about $900 billion in 1986) made it almost impossible to feed the hungry around the world. The commission cited the powerful words of Pope John Paul II in his first encyclical: " 'We all know well that the areas of misery and hunger on our globe could have been made fertile in a short time if the gigantic investments for armaments at the service of war and destruction had been changed into investments at the service of life.' "

The present predicament of the developing nations might well have been different if the United Nations covenants on political and economic rights had not been separated. Both of these documents came into force as a part of international law in 1976. But the United States has never as a working principle accorded equal status to these treaties. In *Basic Rights, Subsistence, Affluence and*

U.S. Foreign Policy Professor Henry Shue pointed out that United States diplomats at the UN in the 1960s and 1970s urged that the single list of rights in the Universal Declaration of Human Rights be "separated into two independently ratifiable treaties" sharply divided into political and economic rights. Professor Shue contended that the United States State Department has continued that dichotomy and in essence has declared that all economic rights, "no matter how vital their fulfillment," are "less genuine rights with less binding duties" than political rights. Criticizing "the intellectual bankruptcy of the presuppositions" of that position, Professor Shue demonstrated that there is no basis in morality, law, or United Nations traditions for any distinction between economic and political rights. They are inseparable by all of the norms of logic, law, and justice.

Professor Shue recommended that Section 502B (forbidding all economic or military aid to nations with a pattern of human rights abuses) be amended to apply to those nations that fail to honor the right to food, housing, and education. If that particular priority had been operational in the 1970s the United States might not have helped the Shah to purchase sophisticated weapons when nutrition and education were neglected in Iran.

The appalling presence of hunger in the world has always bothered Americans. They see such a state of things as unnecessary, correctable, and unacceptable. In 1976, after extensive hearings, the United States Congress enacted a resolution stating "the need to combat hunger shall be a fundamental point of reference in the formulation and implementation of United States policy in all areas that bear on hunger." Congress reaffirmed "the right of every person at home and abroad to food and a nutritionally adequate diet." The resolution urged that the "United States should increase substantially its assistance for self-help development among the poorest people of the world with particular emphasis on increasing food production." This resolution, along with other national and international commitments, affords substantial evidence that the United States has committed itself to the idea of a right to food.

To put the need of a child or an adult for food into the language of law and human rights could almost seem to be callous. The need for food is so self-evident; why must the complex language of law and lawyers be used to justify it? The answer is of course that often the moral claims of one generation become the legal rights of the next generation. The world is in all probability more morally committed to the elimination of hunger than ever before. The emphasis on the right to food has been successful to some extent. Since 1960 forty–one nations have ended mass hunger within their borders; the most dramatic case is China. Yet the food shortage remains a crisis. A letter for support from UNICEF expresses anguish at the death of children in these touching words: "No statistic can express what it's like to see even one child die that way . . . to see a mother sitting hour after hour, leaning her child's body against her own . . . to watch the small feeble head movements that expend all the energy a youngster has left . . . to see the panic in a dying tot's innocent eyes . . . and then to know in a moment that life is gone."

Problems related to food on a global scale are infinitely complex and often baffling. But the human rights resolution over the past forty years has recognized the right to food as the right without which no other right is attainable. Western nations and the United States have, perhaps inadvertently or carelessly, underemphasized the right to food in their exaltation of the political privileges so cherished in democratic nations. But the right of everyone to a nutritionally adequate diet must take precedence over all other rights.

15. Religion and the Future of Human Rights

As one surveys the surge—indeed the explosion—of human rights laws and activities over the last forty years, one has to ask whether the overall level of public morality has been improved. The question is cosmic and probably unanswerable. But one of the many factors to be considered is the potential long-range consequences of the aspirations that have become a part of international law since the establishment of the United Nations. Genocide, torture, totalitarianism, political detention, racism, the oppression of women, and massive malnutrition may still be tragically present in the universe. But have moral forces been launched that will eventually abate or abolish these abuses of human rights? The broader question is of course whether any moral force has ever had any permanent effect on man's morality since Cain killed Abel. To answer this question we must contemplate how much worse things would be if moral laws had not been vigorously advanced through the centuries by spiritual leaders, jurists, legislators, and individuals with humanitarian instincts.

One of the central global forces for a higher personal and public morality is, of course, religion. The Charter of the United Nations required all signatory nations to pledge to promote human rights without distinction as to race, sex, language, or religion. The Universal Declaration of Human Rights and the International Bill of Rights followed the same approach, adding the right to freedom of thought and conscience to those conditions that may not be made the basis for any invidious discrimination.

But understandably the goal of eliminating all intolerance and discrimination based on religion or belief was perhaps the most difficult and intractable of all of the aspirations of the United Nations. It was not until November 25, 1981, that the United Nations General Assembly was able to agree on the Declaration on the Elimination of All Forms of Intolerance and of Discrimination Based on Religion and Belief. And then the final document was not a covenant or a treaty to be ratified by all nations but only an article for informal agreement and common aspiration.

THE UNITED NATIONS DECLARATION ON RELIGIOUS TOLERANCE

The declaration on religious tolerance seems to be more a Western document than the other covenants and treaties issued by the United Nations. The document exalts tolerance and freedom of religion. Every child, for example, is guaranteed the "right to have access to education in the matter of religion or belief in accordance with the wishes of his parents." He or she shall, moreover, "not be compelled to receive teaching on religion or belief against the wishes of his parents." Other specific rights are protected. All may observe days of rest and celebrate holidays in accordance with their religious traditions. The declaration notes that denial of the right to freedom of thought, conscience, and religion has "brought, directly or indirectly, wars and great suffering to mankind." The UN General Assembly obviously does not feel called upon to analyze or resolve the reasons why religions have done things that, in the words of the declaration, amount to "kindling hatred between peoples and nations." The UN document urges only that there be "understanding, tolerance and respect in matters relating to freedom of religion and belief." The norm for the conduct of religious groups is that they do not use religion "for ends inconsistent with the Charter of the United Nations" and its purposes and principles.

Is this a norm that has enough clarity and consistency to make a difference? Would Moslem nations, Protestant and Catholic forces in Belfast, or militantly anti-Communist nations like the United States be likely to come to the conclusion that they cannot impose their religious views on others if in so doing they violate some of the principles of the United Nations? One hopes that the answer would be affirmative, but it is much too soon to try to assess whatever impact the 1981 UN statement on religious freedom might have.

Nations do have an escape clause in the declaration if they are looking for one. Article 1 states that the freedom to manifest one's religion "may be subject only to such limitations as are pre-scribed by law and are necessary to protect public safety, order, health or morals or the fundamental rights and freedoms of others." A nation seeking to discourage dissidence or to repress an unpopular religion can easily find lawyers who will reconcile its conduct with the exception provided for in this article of the UN declaration. But the document is as firm as could be expected when it is remembered that it is the product of nations where the dominant religions include Christianity, Judaism, Buddhism, Hinduism, and others.

A militant for a particular religion could persuasively argue that the UN declaration on religious tolerance subordinates religious belief to the secular objectives of the United Nations. These people could even argue that the document gives a certain priority to secular objectives, since the document in effect prohibits civil rulers from making any decisions concerning human rights based exclusively on religion: "Discrimination between human beings on grounds of religion or belief constitutes an affront to human dignity and a disavowal of the principles of the Charter of the United Nations." Aggressive proponents of a particular religion could feel that this approach removes religion from its rightful place at the core and center of society.

The problems the United Nations faced in 1981 when it finally agreed, in a series of compromises, to this consensus statement on religious discrimination are comparable to the dilemmas faced by twenty-three hundred Catholic bishops at the Second Vatican Council in 1965. The bishops fashioned their famous statement setting aside the long-held traditional doctrine of the Catholic church, that allowed and even required it to favor the establishment of the Catholic church as the official religion in nations where it was the majority religion. The seminal principles favoring religious freedom adopted by Vatican II are the same as in the 1981 UN document on religion, although the UN statement grounds its primary premises more on human rights than does the Vatican II declaration.

It cannot really be denied that the UN declaration on religious tolerance tends to privatize religion. In the event of a clash between a religious group and a nonreligious group, it declares that the principle of tolerance should be supreme. That of course has not been a priority followed by all religions. Nor would some religions agree to it now. As a result some militant religious sects around the world may reject the attitudes and approach of the declaration. Moslems could argue that the UN declaration tolerates and even exalts indifference and that as a result it undermines the very foundation of national and international law and morality. Strong anti-Communists may feel that the UN declaration on religious tolerance condones rather than condemns the Soviet war on religion. And secularists may feel that the UN declaration is replete with loopholes that allow religious zealots to justify the repression of disbelievers or dissidents. But the 1981 UN declaration may be the best possible compromise between 160 nations that represent at least a dozen major world religions.

The UN document does raise essential and probably unsolvable questions. Does it seek to create a certain supermorality outside of formal religious structures? Does it tend to paper over the profound cultural and political differences in the approach of various nations to the role of religion in forming the morality of a nation? Does it minimize the importance of these differences by clearly suggesting that they have to be subordinated to or sublimated by the ideal of tolerance and understanding?

The United States clearly had an immense influence on the formation of the UN charter and the international human rights covenants. The United States Declaration of Independence and the first ten amendments to the United States Constitution are reflected in the charter and the covenants that for the first time in history internationalize the aspirations of Western democratic states. The UN declaration on religious tolerance also reflects the separation of church and state mandated in the United States Constitution. The First Amendment forbids an established state religion but maximizes the free exercise of religion or irreligion. To some extent that is the underlying formula of the UN declaration on religious tolerance. The UN document does not expressly forbid a state-sponsored religion, but it strongly advocates tolerance and expressly forbids any discrimination on the basis of religion or belief.

Can such a formula, applied throughout the world, allow the diverse religions to flourish and in so doing create the necessary moral support to ensure the acceptance of enforcement of a wide range of human rights? Or does the denial of an official status to any organized religion tend to inhibit that religion so that it will not radiate those moral and spiritual values that are, by everyone's admission, indispensable for the successful enforcement of internationally recognized human rights?

These are the questions that will be asked more and more, especially by the Moslem nations, where religion and government and law and morality are interwoven and inseparable in ways almost unknown to Western nations. In the literature on human rights, at least up to this date, however, there is no discernible strong rejection of the entire set of presuppositions on which the UN human rights covenants are grounded. Nations that have inherited Anglo-American or common law from the British Commonwealth, such as India, feel confortable with the international covenants even though they were fashioned in large part by the former colonial powers. African nations are less comfortable, but the UN covenants are not substantially dissimilar from the civil law or the Napoleonic Code Belgium, France and Portugal brought to some African countries. The nations of Asia theoretically feel less kinship with the premises and principles of the new international human rights law, but again there are no strong protests from scholars or jurists in Asian lands. The millions living in nations that were once colonies to European countries have to recognize that their liberation from the domination of a foreign power came about because of the acceptance everywhere of the human rights and fundamental freedoms set forth in the documents of the United Nations.

RELIGIOUS PRINCIPLES AND HUMAN RIGHTS

The deepest and firmest conviction of those who drafted the international human rights covenants was that there is a common and universal set of moral principles known or knowable to all human beings. The Catholic tradition has for centuries called that tradition the natural moral law and has defined it as a participation by humanity in the eternal law rooted in God Himself. Jurists and others perceive that tradition as deriving from the universal respect men have or should have for the voice of conscience. Others would describe the moral assumptions underlying the covenant on international human rights in somewhat different terms. But among the diverse nations there is some kind of consensus that accepts, or at least does not reject, the premises and the principles on which the UN human rights covenants rest.

But one has to ask, Is this consensus the result of the religious traditions of these nations or has it arisen despite or contrary to those religious traditions? Equally important, can the contents of the international covenants on human rights endure if the religious tradition of a nation or religion is fundamentally opposed to it on, for example, the role of women in society or the way in which political dissidents are treated?

During the forty years in which the international human rights covenants developed, few took the time to think of these profound and troubling questions. In addition, they were not pressing questions, since the covenants did not become a part of world law until 1976. The hope was and is that all the religious and moral traditions of the world would continue to articulate their viewpoints and somehow from all the different sounds a world symphony would be created. No one can say with much finality whether that symphony is in the process of being created. But the dream and vision of the framers of the international covenants continues to be inspiring. The primary promises and pledges now contained in world law inspire the humiliated, the marginalized, the dispossessed, and the alienated. If they are angry, they think of fighting for their rights. If they are witnessing the degradation of other human beings by despots, they feel apprehension, anxiety, and a determination to rise up against tyranny.

But can a worldwide morality and jurisprudence with respect to human rights come to have a paramount influence when the human rights in question rest not on theology or any organized religion but only on the rational commitments that all men are equal and should have equality and justice? Throughout history it has almost always been assumed that the ultimate and permanent basis of the morality of a nation must rest on religion and be agreed to by the vast majority of citizens. Except possibly for the United States—although one could argue that the United States from 1790 to about 1950 was a de facto pan-Protestant nation—nations have ground their public morality on the fundamental religions, ethnic, or cultural roots of the people.

But perhaps even that deep-rooted tradition has to be deemed an anachronism in a world where sovereign nations themselves may in many ways be anachronisms. In any event the international bill of rights has bypassed the idea that all human rights derive from the morality or mystique of individual nation-states. Instead it has proclaimed a wide variety of economic and political rights as absolute, transcending any particular nation's moral or legal priorities. It is a revolution seeking to change something fundamental in the way that nations have operated. It is a magnificent and beautiful experiment. Its feasibility and its predictable success cannot be said to be very clear at this time. But the establishment in times past of a set of rules or laws like the Code of Hammurabi, the Justinian Code, the Magna Carta, or the United States Bill of Rights has eventually had an enormous impact. There are consequently many reasons to think that the promulgation of the international covenants on human rights, while seemingly an act that could be perceived as naive and unrealistic, may be one of the most important events in the history of the world.

But there may be a surprisingly clear and coherent consensus in the family of nations about the nature and enforceability of human rights. A review of some systems of law tend to confirm the idea that the framers of the international bill of rights were not just dreamers or superidealists; they were building on persistent and profound strands in the history of jurisprudence in the West and in other cultures.

In 1968 UNESCO, to celebrate the International Human Rights Year, published a collection of texts gleaned from different cultural traditions that illustrates the historical and cultural universality of human rights. The title, *The Birthright of Man*, reflects the idea that the struggle for human rights is as old as history itself. The desire to protect the individual from the abuse of power by a monarch, a tyrant, or the state has its roots in the traditions and faith of India, China, Japan, Persia, Russia, and other nations.

The perennial conflict between the positive law of the sovereign and the unwritten law of the gods or of nature is seen in its classic form in the Antigone of Sophocles, where respect for the dead and the love of a brother transcend whatever the king might order. In the Code of Hammurabi, two thousand years before

Christ, a monarch records that his mission is "to make justice reign in the kingdom, to destroy the wicked and the violent, to prevent the strong from opposing the weak . . . to enlighten the country and promote the good of the people." In the Middle Ages Thomas Aquinas developed the concept of natural moral law, which has been the matrix for ideas about inalienable, indefeasible, and inprescribable human rights.

Religious belief strengthens and deepens the commitment of many in the human rights movement today. Christians see in the face and agony of every human being the suffering of Christ Himself. The person who suffers is carrying out the mysterious mandate of St. Paul that all of us must somehow make up what is wanting in the sufferings of Christ. For the Christian who believes in the identification of every person with the humanity of the Son of God, the sufferings of that person will be a part of the redemption of the world. A brother or sister in Christ whose human rights are violated is a co-redeemer of the human race, an agent for the sanctification of Christ's Church and, as a child of God, chosen in the unfathomable ways of divine providence to bear witness in ways that he or she may never comprehend.

While this theology of suffering may at first seem to promote a certain indifference to the violation of human rights, it should not, when correctly understood, lead to a passive acceptance of the brutalities that individuals and governments inflict on innocent human beings. Properly interpreted the Christian mysticism about suffering should galvanize Christians to action because it is not merely human beings who suffer, it is Christ Himself. It is literally true that if human sin and suffering had been less, Christ's sufferings in the agony in the garden would have been less. At that moment Christ perceived all the abuses of human beings that would occur through the centuries and he suffered personally for them. Consequently if people can now diminish the level and number of affronts and abuses to the brother and sisters of Christ, His suffering will be diminished.

Human rights activists operating in a secularized atmosphere do not make appeal to a theology or even to a philosophy of human rights. They operate on those principles and values of humanitarianism and idealism universally accepted in modern society. The law contained in the UN covenants is based on assumptions shared by the vast majority of humanity. It is further agreed that if these laws were strictly enforced, the abuse of human rights would be sharply curtailed. Some observers may wonder if these assumptions are adequate to the tasks involved. But the worldwide consensus that the observance of human rights should be improved is pervasive. And it is self-evident that the human rights movement can only be strengthened if it is buttressed by theological and philosophical underpinnings.

Those who believe in the Judeo-Christian tradition and perhaps the believers in any of the world's religions may urge that law will not be effective without love. They are right. Love, the capacity to subordinate one's own selfish interest to the good of others, is essential. But law that can be defined as the enforcement of human rights is the operating arm of love. Law is a feeble instrument even if it is strong and is buttressed by effective sanctions. Without love law has to rely on sheer threat; law in those circumstances will be evaded, avoided, or ridiculed.

MEETING THE CHALLENGE OF THE FUTURE

The dream of human rights appears to many to be utopian and almost unattainable. One of the major reasons human rights are not being enforced is the buildup in arms since the end of World War II. The rise in the number of military governments adversely affects human rights since military-controlled governments are more than twice as likely as other Third World governments to make frequent use of torture and other violent forms of repression. In 1986 more than half of the military governments in the world made frequent use of torture, brutality, disappearances, and political killings to intimidate their citizens.

In 1986, the International Year of Peace, global military expenditures reached $900 billion. Extravagant military expenditures are a major reason why in 1986 at least one billion people were inadequately housed, every third adult could not read or write, and one person in five lived in gnawing poverty. The hemorrhage of resources consumed for arms means that a Hiroshima-like catastrophe occurs every three days—120,000 children die unnecessarily. The direct casualties of war are equally appalling. According to Ruth Leger Sivard's *World Military and Social Expen-*

ditures, in World War I 19.6 million people were killed; in World War II, 38.3 million were killed. Since 1945 another 25 million have lost their lives in military conflicts. The Unites States, in its role as the moral architect of the UN charter and human rights covenants, certainly gave a creative impetus to human rights law and idealism. But in the decades during which the United States has largely resisted the ratification of the UN treaties, it has established three hundred major military installations abroad, covering 2 million acres with 474,170 United States military personnel overseas, not including 250,000 United States military personnel afloat.

The East-West gridlock is central and crucial to the future of human rights. Andrei Sakharov put it well in 1985: "Peace, progress, human rights—these three goals are indissolubly linked; it is impossible to achieve one if the others are ignored."

In the 1980s a commission chaired by Willy Brandt studied the need for a new international order. In its report the commission concluded that it is not the lack of technical resources that prevents the challenge from being met but the fact that the necessary political decisions "will not be possible without a global consensus *on the moral plane* that the basis of any world or national order must be people and respect for the individual's rights, as defined in the Universal Declaration of Human Rights. Only if those ideas are sincerely accepted by governments, *and especially by individuals,* will the political decisions be possible and viable" (emphasis added).

The quality of a society can be judged, Lord Moulton wrote, by its obedience to the unenforceable. In the past human rights were not even defined as enforceable by the world community. But now for the first time since humanity invented law there is a plea for the internationalization of those fundamental rules or aspirations common to all people. Even if all the human rights initiatives undertaken by the family of nations over the last two generations became miraculously effective, human kind would not return to some lost paradise. But the implementation of human rights would be a way of curbing and civilizing all the brutish activities that derive from that primordial sin.

Americans have a unique and very special role to play in the human rights revolution. America, more than any other nation, led the way to the formation of the United Nations and the development of the twenty or more major treaties of that organization. The United States transmitted the moral and philosophical bases of its own governmental institutions to the family of nations. So the United States has a daunting moral, legal, and political duty to verify and enhance the transcendence of human rights. George Santayana said it well: "Being an American is in and of itself almost a moral condition." Another American, the poet and lawyer Archibald MacLeish, epitomized the mandate of America in these words: "There are those who will say that the liberation of humanity, the freedom of man and mind are nothing but a dream. They are right. It is a dream. It is the American dream."

List of Major Human Rights Documents

Document	Issuing Body	Date
American Convention on Human Rights	Organization of American States	11/22/69
American Declaration of the Rights and Duties of Man	Organization of American States	5/2/48
Charter of the United Nations	United Nations	12/9/48
Convention on the Prevention and Punishment of the Crime of Genocide	United Nations	12/9/48
European Convention for the Protection of Human Rights and Fundamental Freedoms	Council of Europe	11/4/50
International Convention on the Elimination of All Forms of Discrimination against Women	United Nations	12/18/79
International Convention on the Elimination of All Forms of Racial Discrimination	United Nations	3/7/66
International Covenant on Civil and Political Rights	United Nations	12/16/66
International Covenant on Economic, Social, and Cultural Rights	United Nations	12/16/66
Optional Protocol to the International Covenant on Civil and Political Rights	United Nations	12/16/66
Standard Minimum Rules for the Treatment of Prisoners	United Nations	7/31/57

Universal Declaration of Human Rights	United Nations	12/10/48
African Charter on Human and Peoples' Rights	Organization of African Unity	6/1981
Convention on the Political Rights of Women	United Nations	3/31/53
Declaration on the Elimination of All Forms of Intolerance and of Discrimination Based on Religion and Belief	United Nations	11/25/81
Convention against Torture and Other Cruel, Inhuman, or Degrading Treatment or Punishment	United Nations	12/10/84

Select Bibliography

American Academy of Arts and Science. *Daedalus—Human Rights.* Cambridge: American Academy of Arts and Sciences, 1983.

Amnesty International. *Torture in the Eighties.* London: Amnesty International Publications, 1984.

Brown, Peter G., and Douglas MacLean. *Human Rights and U.S. Foreign Policy.* Lexington: D. C. Heath and Company, 1979.

Columbia University. Center for the Study of Human Rights. *Human Rights: A Topical Bibliography.* Boulder: Westview Press, 1983.

Franck, Thomas M. *Human Rights in Third World Perspective.* 3 vols. New York: Oceana Publications, 1982.

Human Rights Quarterly (November 1986). Baltimore: Johns Hopkins University Press.

Kammers, Donald P., and Gilburt D. Loescher, eds. *Human Rights and American Foreign Policy.* Notre Dame: University of Notre Dame Press, 1979.

Lillich, Richard B., and Frank C. Newman. *International Human Rights: Problems of Law and Policy.* Boston: Little, Brown & Company, 1979.

Nanda, Ved P., James R. Scarritt, and George W. Shepherd. *Global Human Rights: Public Policies, Comparative Measures, and NGO Strategies.* Boulder: Westview Press, Inc., 1981.

Robertson, A. H. *Human Rights in the World.* New York: St. Martin's Press, 1982.

Schoultz, Lars. *Human Rights and United States Policy toward Latin America.* Princeton: Princeton University Press, 1981.

Shue, Henry. *Basic Rights: Subsistence, Affluence and U.S. Foreign Policy.* Princeton: Princeton University Press, 1980.

Sidorsky, David, ed. *Essays on Human Rights: Contemporary Issues and Jewish Perspectives.* Philadelphia: The Jewish Publication Society of America, 1979.

Sieghart, Paul. *The Lawful Rights of Mankind.* Oxford: Oxford University Press, 1985.

United Nations. *The United Nations and Human Rights.* New York: United Nations Publication, 1978.

U.S. Presidential Commission on World Hunger. *Overcoming World Hunger: The Challenge Ahead.* Washngton, D.C.: GPO, 1980.

Vogelgesang, Sandy. *American Dream, Global Nightmare: The Dilemma of U.S. Human Rights Policy.* New York: W. W. Norton and Company, 1980.

Index